MICHAEL

Четверг.

10. | 27.

12;

MICHAEL

The unofficial and unauthorised biography of
MICHAEL JACKSON
by Duane Harewood

Published by
Kandour Ltd
1-3 Colebrook Place
London N1 8HZ

This edition printed in 2004 for
Bookmart Limited
Registered Number 2372865
Trading as Bookmart Ltd
Blaby Road
Wigston
Leicester LE18 4SE

First published June 2004

ISBN 1–904756–08-5

Production services:
Metro Media Ltd

Author: Duane Harewood

With thanks to: Jenny Ross, Emma Hayley,
Lee Coventry & Belinda Weber

Cover design: Mike Lomax
Cover Image: Rex Features

Inside Images: Rex Features

© Kandour Ltd

Printed and bound by Nørhaven Paperback, Denmark

MICHAEL JACKSON

FOREWORD

This series of biographies is a celebration of celebrity. It features some of the world's greatest modern-day icons including movie stars, soap personalities, pop idols, comedians and sporting heroes. Each biography examines their struggles, their family background, their rise to stardom and in some cases their struggle to stay there. The books aim to shed some light on what makes a star. Why do some people succeed when others fail?

Written in a light-hearted and lively way, and coupled with the most up-to-date details on the world's favourite heroes and heroines, this series is an entertaining read for anyone interested in the world of celebrity. Discover all about their career highlights – what was the defining moment to propel them into superstardom? No story about fame is without its ups and downs. We reveal the emotional rollercoaster ride that many of these stars have been on to stay at the top. Read all about your most adored personalities in these riveting books.

MICHAEL JACKSON

CONTENTS

MICHAEL JACKSON

FACTFILE

Full Name: Michael Joseph Jackson

Eye Colour: Brown

Date of Birth: Friday, 29 August 1958

Place of Birth: Gary, Indiana, U.S.A

Height: 5' 10"

Marriages:

Lisa Marie Presley 18 May 1994 – 18 January 1996

Debbie Rowe 15 November 1996 – 8 October 1999

Children:

Son: Prince Michael born 13 February 1997,
mother Debbie Rowe

Daughter: Paris Katherine Michael born on 3rd April
1998, mother Debbie Rowe

Son: Prince Michael II, born 2002 to surrogate
mother undisclosed. His nickname is 'Blanket'

Star sign: Virgo (22 August- 21 September)

Virgo's virtues include a sharp and probing intellect. They have a tendency to be perfectionists and agonise over the smallest of details. For them structure and precision is all-important. They are constantly striving to improve themselves and situations around them. Virgo's on the whole also tend to be shy, gentle characters that share a love of nature and animals. Other famous Virgo's are, Sean Connery, Richard Gere and Raquel Welch.

MICHAEL JACKSON

FACTFILE

Chinese birth sign: Dog:
Like their four legged name sakes the are devouted and popular. They will always be there for their friends and family when they are called upon. They like their privacy and will fight to protect it. They are not a pretentious bunch and don't like that trait in others. They can sum up other people fairly quickly.

Career High: Dominating the music scene throughout the Eighties when *Thriller* became the largest selling album of all time. In 1984 he received eight Grammies, the most that anyone has ever had in one year.

Father: Joseph Walter
Mother: Katherine Esther
Brothers and sisters:
Maureen (Rebbie) 29 May 1950
Sigmund Esco (Jackie) 4 May 1951
Tariano Adaryl (Tito) 15 October 1953
Jermaine LaJuane 11 December 1954
LaToya Yvonne 29 May 1956
Marlon David 12 March 1957 twin
Brandon 12 March 1957 twin died within 24hrs of birth
Steven Randall (Randy) 29 October 1961
Janet Dameta 16 May 1966

1

Introduction

MICHAEL JACKSON

INTRODUCTION

F riday 29 August 1958 was not a special day in Gary, Indiana, and indeed Gary, was far from being a special place. Like many predominantly poor black neighbourhoods in Fifties America, things did not bode well for its future. But it was on this day and in this location that the world's greatest entertainer was to be born, Michael Joseph Jackson.

The impact that this boy was destined to have on the world of entertainment could never have been estimated, so his humble beginnings make his story all the more remarkable.

Here we celebrate Jackson's extraordinary

MICHAEL JACKSON

INTRODUCTION

talents, and plot the defining events over his 40-year career. The King of Pop's journey began with a primary school in front of classmates. Today he commands stadiums of thousands and television audiences of millions. Michael Jackson was part of the original and best-ever boy-band, the Jackson Five, and signed to the legendary Motown Records Label. Michael watched and learned from some of soul music's finest performers. This early success was nothing to what he would achieve when he decided to leave his brothers behind and go solo.

His *Thriller* album firmly established Michael as a living legend smashing records and setting new goals by selling over 56 million copies. He consistently outsells every other artist on the planet. Currently worth an estimated $300 million, his innovation heightened our expectations and set new musical standards by which all other others would be judged. This book explores the man behind the myth, and gives an understanding of what drives this special entertainer.

So, what makes him so driven? What were his earliest influences? What tricks does he use to keep his audience spellbound?

His popularity transcends age, race and colour. His unique style and ability has made him

INTRODUCTION

the most famous person on the planet.

In 1993, there was an event that was to rock Jackson's world. His friendship with a 12-year-old boy and the subsequent allegations resulted in a lawsuit, a fall in record sales and a long road to recovery. Two marriages, three children and 10 years later there is a feeling of déja vu as Jackson again has to deal with more controversy. Without doubt, 2004 will prove to be the most important year in the singer's life. Now, his future hangs in the balance. Whatever the future holds for Jackson, his past is secured, there has never been and there will never again be anything quite like Michael Jackson.

2

2300 Jackson Street

2300 JACKSON STREET

Thirty miles south-east of Chicago, on the shores of Lake Michigan, there's an industrial city called Gary. Founded in 1906 on a lakeside wilderness, by the US Steel Corporation, it remains relatively unknown outside the States. Steel production sustained the economy and provided employment for the local populace. Today, Gary is enjoying a long-term, well overdue makeover, but when newly weds Joseph and Katherine Jackson settled there in 1949, it was a rather grim place. The whole area was dominated by the steel industry; its factories belched out smoke across the skyline, which could be seen all the way from Chicago. Joe was a crane driver at the steel mill, while his wife worked part-time in the local branch of Sears Roebuck department store. The couple's fortunes fluctuated, mirroring the global steel market of the time.

Joe and Katherine bought their first house, situated on the corner of West 23rd and Jackson Street – auspiciously named, but after former US President Andrew Jackson. However, it is with our family that this street will be associated forever. Number 2300 was a detached, two bedroomed bungalow, which would become Michael's first home. It was later immortalised in the Jackson's 1989 ballad, *2300 Jackson Street*.

Maureen Reilette (aka Rebbie) was their first-born child, she bounced into the world on 29 May 1950. A year later, 4 May 1951, their first son Sigmund Esco (aka Jackie) was born. The couple then had a bit of a breather, before Katherine gave birth to Tariano Adaryl (aka Tito) on 15 October 1953. The following year saw the arrival of Jermaine LaJuane, by now the family seemed to be running short on nicknames. LaToya Yvonne followed in May, with Marlon David putting in an appearance less then a year later.

Marlon was a twin, but sadly his brother

2300 JACKSON STREET

Brandon died the day after his birth. On Friday, 29 August 1958 Michael Joseph the baby of pop emerged. After a short break from maternity, Katherine gave birth to Steven Randall (aka Randy) on 29 October 1961 and five years later, in May 1966 Janet Dameta entered the world to complete entertainment's most famous family.

In the Sixties there was a sharp downturn in the steel industry, which hit the Gary community particularly hard. As production went down, unemployment and crime went up. People began leaving the area in search of work, abandoning their properties in various states of disrepair. As a result it became an increasingly rough neighbourhood. Katherine was afraid that her family, particularly the boys, could end up running with the wrong crowd. She had always been a religious lady, and took comfort in her faith. As a devout Jehovah's Witness she ensured that every Sunday her children attended the local Kingdom Hall, the Jehovah Witness's place of worship. Michael in particular was taken by the teachings that include: no blood transfusions, celebrations of birthdays or Christmas. Even as an adult Michael would go from door-to-door evangelising and distributing

Watchtower literature. Michael finally left the organisation at the age of 29. Joe Jackson did not share his wife's passion for religion, as his passion was music.

In the early Fifties Joe played guitar with his brother Luther in an R&B band called the Falcons. They managed to get a few local gigs, but that big break eluded them. As money became tighter, Joe abandoned any personal hopes of musical fame for more conventional toil. He worked shifts, managing to hold down two jobs simultaneously. As a result he spent a great deal of time away from home. His precious guitar was relegated to the back of the wardrobe, strictly out of bounds to the children. Tito, like his father, had a good ear and he would sometimes watch the Falcons rehearsing. Tito took advantage of his father's absence and secretly practised with the cherished instrument accompanied by Jackie and Jermaine singing along. One day while jamming, Tito broke a string and as he wasn't able to replace it, his secret was blown. Tito anxiously awaited his father's return. "I knew I was in trouble...we were all in trouble. Our father was strict and we were scared of him."

Needless to say, Joe was not a happy man, at first he chastised his son. But eventually Joe gave

2300 JACKSON STREET

Tito the opportunity to show him what he could do. The months of practising must have paid off, because Joe was genuinely impressed by what he heard. Shortly after this, seeing the potential, Joe bought his son his very own electric guitar. With Tito strumming away, Jackie and Jermaine singing, the little-known and fairly short-lived Jackson Three was formed. Even at this early stage Joe could see that the boys' talents might be their ticket out of Gary.

Joe encouraged his boys to rehearse regularly, sometimes twice a day before and after school. Shortly before his sixth birthday Marlon joined the band. Katherine was pleased that the family were all working together. With the boys occupied inside the house, there was little chance that they would be tempted to mix with the wrong crowd outside. Possibly spurred on by the amount of fun his brothers were having, Michael started to display his own abilities. When he was at primary school, Garnett Elementary, he performed an inspiring heart-rending version of *Climb Every Mountain* from *The Sound of Music*. This was technically his first public appearance. Michael's confidence and ability were astonishing for one so young. He was delighted when he joined his brothers at the age of five, to complete the line-up and the Jacksons, always a close knit family, felt even more united.

Michael took over from Jermaine as the lead vocalist of the Jackson Brothers. His ability to mimic would hold him in good stead, at first copying his brothers and later borrowing moves from soul legends such as James Brown who he used to watch avidly on television.

The band entered their first-ever talent contest, held at the Roosevelt High School gym in 1965; this also happened to be the school that Maureen, Tito and Jermaine attended. The brothers performed a couple of numbers, including the soul classic *My Girl* by The Temptations. This cemented a convincing victory for them and won every heart in the crowd, plus the competition. The brothers continued to practise relentlessly, and began to enter more local talent contests. Annihilating the opposition, they quickly acquired a formidable reputation along with a mantelpiece full of trophies. Children would often gather outside 2300 Jackson Street to listen to the rehearsals, and 'offer' critical comments and suggestions along with the occasional stone through the open windows. The family was a little bit alienated partly because of their unyielding practice sessions, and partly because of their Jehovah Witness affiliations. In a predominantly Baptist and Christian community, the Jacksons stood out. Standing out from the masses didn't upset the family. They knew that they were different; they knew that they were special. These fledgling performances were an early training ground for Michael, he was able to learn how to work the crowd, he was cheeky, cute and the audiences lapped it all up.

The boys played their first paid gig at Mr Lucky's Lounge in Gary; the nightclub also hosted comedians and strippers, it was a full house that night. Joe was paid the princely sum of $5 for his sons' premiere professional performance. But the cash that the audience threw on to the stage more than supplemented the miserly fee, although Michael was never really that concerned with the money he was making, spending most of his share on candy and ice cream for children in the neighbourhood. This was to be pivotal moment for Joe, he realised that this business alone could support his family. He invested just about all of his time and money into the band. He arranged all of their gigs, supervised the rehearsals, dictated the presentational style and transported them around in a Volkswagen campervan to various venues in

2300 JACKSON STREET

Gary and Chicago. With Joe managing and Katherine making the costumes this truly was a family driven business. During this period two other boys became permanent fixtures in the band. Johnny Jackson, not related but referred to as a "cousin", was installed as the group's resident drummer, and Ronny Rancifer took up a place behind the keyboards.

It was at about this time that the Jackson Brothers were renamed the much more catchy, Jackson Five. The idea for the name didn't come from within the family, it was from a female neighbour, and she suggested it after seeing the brothers perform. The family also became regulars on the Chitlin Circuit. This was a phrase used to describe a string of venues, nightclubs, bars and theatres spread throughout the country in pre-Civil Rights America, which catered for black musicians and audiences, when they had previously been unwelcome at other white only clubs. It was essential for un-established black acts to get on to this circuit. For the boys this enabled them to reach a wider audience, travelling mostly at weekends to venues in Cleveland, Baltimore, Ohio and Washington. Working late into the night, the boys would arrive back to Gary in the early hours of the morning, snatching a few hours sleep before getting up for school. Although the boys enjoyed what they were doing, they had a hectic schedule of performances and rehearsals. It was an arduous time, especially for Michael.

Although full of confidence on stage with a vocal maturity that belied his age, Michael was a shy, somewhat introverted child away from the limelight. He didn't always enjoy the venues that they played, sharing the bill with third-rate comedians and washed-up strippers held no interest for him.

The boys didn't have to wait too long before they reached more glamourous heights. The Jackson Five were the support act for the legendary songstress, Gladys Knight along with her Pips, at the Regal Theatre in Chicago. There were some executives from Motown Records in the audience that night, but they did not approach the band on this occasion. The concert did however lead to more work for the boys, supporting other big names such as the O'Jays, James Brown and Jackie Wilson. Michael would observe his heroes from the wings and make mental notes regarding their poise, style and stage presence. He was honing his craft and serving his apprenticeship with some of the best in the business. With that standard of tuition, Michael really began to excel at his art. Even at this early age Michael was the object of unwanted hearsay and speculation. Rumours started circulating that he was in fact "a 35-year-old midget masquerading as a child".

In 1967 the band played the infamous Apollo Theatre in Harlem. The theatre staged an amateur night every Wednesday, and the audiences were notoriously harsh if they didn't enjoy the acts, throwing bottles and cans at the performers. Many good acts had been totally humiliated there and many great acts had launched careers from there. That night the atmosphere was electrifying it was the end of a hot August summer's day. Over 1,400 people were packed into the auditorium, the stifling heat added to the tension. Walking on stage was likened to entering the coliseum, with the crowd baying for blood. The Jackson Five were only too aware of the pressures they were under, Joe did not accept failure as an option, and he had the utmost faith in his children's ability. That night the Jackson Five delivered, they tore the house down, and received a virtually unheard of standing ovation. It was beyond even Joe's wildest expectations. They were to play the venue over and over again; the Jacksons had now entered the musical hall of fame.

The Jackson Five were big in their hometown Gary, they were the city's celebrities, but they needed more national exposure. After seeing the boys strutting their stuff at one of their many neighbourhood appearances, Gordon Keith (aka William Adams) took an interest. Gordon was an entrepreneur. In addition to writing and producing songs, he was the co-owner of a small independent recording label, Steeltown. He was eager to sign the Jackson Five. Joe met with Gordon and Ben Brown (co-owner) to discuss terms and shortly afterwards, the group secured their first-ever record deal. The boys were ecstatic; Michael was only nine-years-old at the time so had already spent nearly half of his life working towards this moment.

The band arrived at Gordon's house, which also doubled as Steeltown Records HQ, early one Saturday morning to cut their first disc. The studio was fairly small and basic, but it did the job. Prior to this, they had not had any studio experience and after the initial excitement found the process a little tedious. At this stage the Jackson Five were very much a live act. Studio work can be very slow and repetitive, not a conducive environment for active young boys. In the spring of 1968, the Jackson Five released their first single, *Big Boy,* a well-produced mid-tempo 'slow groove'. The record received limited distribution, and was aired on the local radio station WWCA. The follow up single was an up-beat number called, *We Don't Have to Be Over 21 (To Fall In Love)*. The Jacksons got a real buzz when they heard their single playing on the radio for the first time.

Pumped-up by their recent record release, the boys returned to the Apollo in Harlem, this time as paid performers. On this occasion an associate producer for *The David Frost Show* saw the group and appreciated how popular they were with the notoriously unforgiving crowd. He immediately signed them to appear on the TV show in New York. Joe, realising what an appearance on network television could lead to, agreed without hesitation. It was too good a chance to miss.

The Jackson Family went into overdrive, rehearsing dance routines, preparing costumes, ensuring that nothing would spoil this once in a lifetime opportunity. They didn't take time off from gigging though, and prior to *The David Frost Show* appearance, they had to fulfil another engagement.

2300 JACKSON STREET

Michael and his brothers were the support act for a band called, Bobby Taylor and the Vancouvers. They travelled to Chicago's High Chaparral Club to attend the concert. Bobby Taylor was so impressed by the Jackson Five's performance that night, that he called Motown Records to try and arrange an audition for them. He got through to Ralph Seltzer an executive at the record company, and pleaded with him. Gladys Knight had also been petitioning the label on behalf of the Jacksons. The pair was successful, and although Ralph had some reservations, he invited the Jackson Five to Detroit for a 'try out'. There was only one slight problem, Motown Records wanted to see the boys on the same day as *The David Frost Show*. They couldn't do both. Joe was faced with one of his most difficult decisions ever, and in the end, the Jackson Five packed up their VW campervan and hit the road to Motown.

3

The Motown years

THE MOTOWN YEARS

he Jackson Five rolled up on West Grand Boulevard outside Motown's Detroit offices on Tuesday, 23 July 1968. Detroit was affectionately known as 'motor city' because of the major car manufacturers based there. The name 'Motown' was derived from motor town. The record label had become synonymous with smash soul hits, and pitched itself as 'the sound of young America'. The label had managed to cross-over selling black music to a mixed audience. Motown founder, Berry Gordy Jnr, was a very ambitious and successful man. Born in 1929, he dropped out of school to become a featherweight boxer, before joining the army where he served in Korea. He was a budding songwriter, and in his time owned three jazz record shops, before working on the production line at the Ford car plant. Singer Al Green invited Gordy to compose a song for Jackie Wilson, and in November 1957 the tune *Reet Petite* hit the charts. With new impetus Berry Gordy left the car factory to become a professional lyric writer and set up his hit factory. By 1959 Gordy had formed a publishing company called Jobete Music, an amalgamation of his children's names, Hazel Joy, Berry and Terry. Gordy went on to set up Motown in order to distribute his music; he also set up other offshoot companies including Hitsville USA (the name given to Motown's recording studios). In April 1961, four years after his initial success with *Reet Petite*, Gordy found suitable premises to base his empire, a two-storey shingle-roofed house with enough room for a studio in the basement. Gordy's family leant him $800, and from that humble start he went on to produce some of the most famous names in black music history – Diana Ross, Mary Wells, The Temptations, Stevie Wonder and Smokey Robinson to name but a few.

The Jacksons desperately wanted to add their chapter to the Motown success story. Ralph

MICHAEL JACKSON

THE MOTOWN YEARS

Seltzer and Suzanne de Passe (Gordy's PA) greeted the Jacksons on that Tuesday morning and informed them that Gordy would not be joining them for the audition. Gordy was in Los Angeles overseeing Motown's relocation to the West Coast. The boss had big plans for his record company; he wanted to expand Motown's interests and branch out into other aspects of show business. The Jacksons' audition was to be filmed for Gordy to view in LA. Gordy had set his company up in the mould of the Hollywood star system. Motown took raw, hungry urban talents and transformed them into polished performers. Taking responsibility for every aspect of their image on and off the stage. The team that Gordy had assembled repackaged potential stars into a highly produced, highly marketable product. Each artist would be nurtured and groomed as necessary with the help of an in-house team ranging from songwriters and producers to the deportment coaches.

That bright morning as the Jacksons prepared to play, they were becoming increasingly aware of what the Motown deal could mean to them. In the past Joe had sent demo tapes into the company, but had never received a reply. As the band set up (consisting of Johnny, Jackie, Tito, Jermaine, Marlon and Michael), a group of record executives gathered in anticipation to see the performance. It was a sterile atmosphere, the band were used to playing in front of appreciative audiences, up for a good night out, not suited-and-booted straight-faced management. Seltzer still had concerns about the young band, and Michael's age in particular. Michael's personality didn't really shine through until he stepped on to a stage. The Jackson Five began their set with a James Brown number. Michael pulled out all the stops, displaying his full repertoire. Dancing and singing his nine-year-old heart out, sliding across the floor and dropping to his knees. The boys ran through a few tried and tested cover versions, and although the executives scribbled down copious notes, they showed no reaction, no applause, no nothing. At the end of the session the Jacksons were no wiser about their future, the record executives faces didn't betray any feelings, either positive or negative. Ralph Seltzer thanked them for attending and the band departed. Joe and his sons left there deflated, Joe probably wondered if missing out on *The David Frost Show* had been a good gamble after all. The only consolation was that the family

THE MOTOWN YEARS

had given it their best shot.

Back home in Gary, the boys had an anxious wait. When the phone eventually rang, it was fantastic news. The boys were invited back to Detroit three days later. Berry Gordy was delighted when he saw the audition tape and wasted no time in signing up the next big thing. At the time Motown had just lost a song-writing team that was at the core of the company's unique sound. Holland-Dozier-Holland (Lamont Dozier, Brian and Eddy Holland), although they sound like a firm of solicitors, the trio were in fact responsible for penning much of the record label's classic tunes. Their extensive back catalogue included *Nowhere to Run*, *Can I Get A Witness*, *How Sweet it is to be Loved by You*, *Standing in the Shadow of Love* and *Baby Love*. The split was a big blow for the 'Motown Family'. The brand needed to appeal to the younger fans and the Jacksons fitted the bill perfectly.

When the family returned to Motown, on Friday, 26 July 1968, they were welcomed like conquering heroes, a complete contrast to their last visit. The boys really felt like they'd arrived. It was time to get the paperwork sorted out. Ralph

MICHAEL JACKSON

THE MOTOWN YEARS

Seltzer presented Joe with a standard seven-year contract. Motown felt that it could take this amount of time to establish an artist and find them a niche. Joe didn't want to commit his sons to such a long deal not wanting them to miss out on other potential opportunities in the future. Joe negotiated with Seltzer, and spoke with Gordy on the phone. Gordy conceded and agreed to let the boys sign for a period of one year. Not being a lawyer, Joe did not fully appreciate the contract that he and his boys signed.

The Motown Record Corporation now owned the name Jackson Five, so they could replace any of the boys with any other artist. Motown were under no obligation to release any of the bands' material and most importantly the Jacksons could not record for any other label until five years after the termination of the contract. Effectively Motown owned the brothers, they were in total control. Motown paid the band a little over 5% in royalties, which was their standard rate. However, when split five ways each boy walked away with approximately 2 cents per album. Berry Gordy displayed shrewd business acumen. The Jacksons also had some unfinished business with Steeltown Records, the

THE MOTOWN YEARS

label that had provided them with their first-ever record deal. Reluctantly, Gordy was eventually forced to buy the brothers out of that existing contract. At the time Joe and the boys were just pleased to be part of the hallowed Motown myth.

In late September, the Jackson Five played their first gig for Motown (not officially) in their hometown of Gary. It was a fund-raising concert on behalf of Mayor Richard Hatcher's political campaign. The event was billed as the 'Soul Weekend'; the Jackson Five opened proceedings and the event featured Gladys Knight and the Pips along with Bobby Taylor and the Vancouver's, the artists who had been championing the Jacksons' cause and were instrumental in the boys' rise to stardom. The Motown PR machine would later state that it was here, during this concert that Diana Ross had discovered the Jacksons and got them signed up to the record label. It was felt that associating the youngsters with the established glamourous diva would help their career.

In actual fact, soul diva Diana Ross met the Jacksons for the first time in December at a Christmas party hosted by the Motown boss. This first meeting between Diana Ross and Michael Jackson was to herald the beginning of a continuing friendship. It was a seriously big bash; all of Motown's top names were there. The event was an opportunity for the Jacksons to meet their 'stable mates' along with Motown's headline act Diana Ross and the Supremes.

Since the Jackson Five signed their long-awaited contract back in the summer, to the outside world, nothing much seemed to be happening with their career. They were nowhere nearer to releasing their first single for Motown. The boys would go to school during the week then travel to Detroit at the weekend to work in the studio. Bobby Taylor was pleased to be assigned as their producer. They recorded songs for their first-ever album, things were going well, but after several months of recording, Gordy still had not heard an original tune worthy of being the first single. Knowing how important their debut on the Motown Label would be, he was prepared to hold out until they delivered the goods. A year after the band successfully auditioned, the boys were getting exasperated. After the initial hype the momentum seemed to be running out. Gordy, a man who always liked to have complete autonomy, was mainly based in Los Angeles overseeing other aspects of his corporation. This meant that he couldn't directly monitor their progress. There was only one solution. Gordy moved the Jackson Five and Joe out to Hollywood. Meanwhile Katherine, little Randy and the girls remained in Gary.

4

California calling

MICHAEL JACKSON

CALIFORNIA CALLING

Life on West Coast California was a far cry from Indiana, to the boys everything seemed better, the sunshine, the 'beautiful people', even the air smelled fresher. With the boys in a local Hollywood motel, Berry Gordy was able to take personal charge. His first job was to get them greater exposure and officially launch the Jackson Five on an unsuspecting public. The 'invitation only' event was to be held at LA's hottest nightclub the Daisy on North Rodeo Drive, Beverly Hills. Diana Ross sent out the personal invitations, in which Michael was described as a sensational eight-year-old. This was to be the Jacksons' first

CALIFORNIA CALLING

introduction to the world of PR and spin. In addition to Motown claiming that Diana Ross had discovered the Jackson Five each member had their age reduced by two years – that's showbiz!

That Monday evening, 11 August 1969, the 300-strong crowd saw Diana Ross introduce Motown's newest signing to the 'world'. They had all been rehearsing hard and their routines were slicker than ever. The audience gave them a long and rapturous reception. The group performed some Motown classics along with a Disney ditty *Zip A Dee Doo Dah*, which was to later appear on their debut album. After their set, the music press did mini-interviews with the boys asking about their ambitions and influences. The boys had been prepped beforehand and schooled in the art of answering reporters' questions, the lads even remembered to only give their stage ages, even when pressed. Their performances both on-and off-stage were impeccable. They were fast and eager to learn. The press fell in love with the Jackson Five and Michael in particular. The following day their reviews were peppered with cute, adorable and sweet. So the boys had wooed the music industry insiders, indulged the media and obeyed their management to the letter, all that was required next was a hit record. Later that month also saw the Jackson Five make their television debut with an appearance at the 1969 Miss Black America Contest.

The Motown production policy was very strict producers produced, writers wrote and artists performed. It was a very formulaic system, the Stock, Aitken and Waterman of its day and by the mid-Sixties Motown was the most successful independent record label in the States. Gordy was desperate to find an appropriate tune for the brothers; money was being spent on their development, studio costs and living expenses etc. The money needed to be recouped from record sales.

Deke Richards, Motown's Creative Director, had been working with Freddie Perren and Fonce Mizell, (collectively christened The Corporation) on a new song originally intended for Gladys Knight and the Pips. However, when they had finished the song, they were so pleased with the results that they were hoping to persuade Motown's first lady Diana Ross to have the tune. When Gordy heard the tune, *I Want To Be Free* he didn't think that it was suitable for Ross but felt that with a little reworking it could be ideal for the Jacksons. Although a good tune, lyrically it didn't match the boys' persona. The team worked hard to give it an appeal to a much younger audience. Richards encountered another problem when Michael began rehearsing the new number. His pronunciation was not precise enough; as a predominately live entertainer he had concentrated mostly on his stage performance rather than his vocal technique. It took a great deal of time to remedy this, but Michael was an enthusiastic pupil. When they had finished recording, Richards played the results to Gordy, but the boss was not impressed, he ordered them back into the studio the following day. The team worked until the early hours of the morning, Michael was falling asleep at his microphone, after about 20 or so takes the job was done, *I Want To Be Free* had become *I Want You Back* and a hit was born. The track would still require some post production before it was ready for the shops a few weeks later, but at last Motown's marketing department had a product to push.

The Jackson Five had been living in various hotels, some more sumptuous than others, since their arrival in California that summer. Suzanne de Passe had been looking after the band's welfare as a hands-on manager, whilst Berry Gordy was more concerned with the bigger picture. Now, in

CALIFORNIA CALLING

October 1969, Berry Gordy took the decision to separate Michael from his family and move him in with Diana Ross at her Hollywood Hills House. Gordy thought that the boy might benefit from being under the wing of an experienced star. Diane Ernestine Ross was only 15 when she joined The Primettes, later to become The Supremes. The diva could sympathise with some of the things that Michael was going through and act as his informal tutor. He was a human sponge observing and absorbing her professionalism and the way she dealt with the pressures of the entertainment industry. During this time, Ross was preparing to leave The Supremes and establish herself as a solo artist. Putting Diana and Michael together would ultimately serve to raise both of their public profiles, another shrewd Motown move.

I Want You Back was finally scheduled for release at the end of October, so there was still time to give the track some much needed pre-publicity. On 18 October 1969, the Jackson Five appeared on ABC's network television show, *The Hollywood Palace*. Diana Ross and The Supremes were hosting the programme that evening and the Jacksons were on the bill with Sammy Davies Jnr. The boys couldn't have asked for a better occasion

CALIFORNIA CALLING

to showcase their talents to a telly audience. Diana Ross introduced the band, and full of energy the boys burst on to the stage and into homes across the length and breadth of America. With their neatly trimmed trademark Afros and their bright psychedelic costumes (wasted on the millions of black and white television sets), they were a breath of fresh air. The studio audience were euphoric and the reactions that the Jacksons received farther afield were also very encouraging.

The next big event for the Jackson Five was a performance on the highly rated and very mainstream *Ed Sullivan Show*, on 14 December 1969. The Sunday night CBS production was a national institution, and was coming to the end of its 16-year run. The programme attracted big names and even bigger ratings. Celebrities such as Buster Keaton, Bob Hope and The Beatles all popped in to see Sullivan at one point or another during his long reign. It was this programme that helped to catapult *I Want You Back* to the number one spot on the Billboard chart, 31 January 1970. The single sold two million copies. Berry Gordy had prophesised that he would get the band three consecutive number one hits; it was beginning to look as though it was not an empty promise. While

CALIFORNIA CALLING

their single was climbing the charts, Motown released the Jackson Five's debut album *Diana Ross Presents The Jackson 5* in December to cash in on the lucrative Christmas market. In addition to containing their rapidly rising single *I Want You Back*, the LP had one other original composition, *Nobody*. The other tunes were familiar standards such as *Zip A Dee Doo Dah, Standing in the Shadow of Love* and *My Cherie Amour*.

By now Michael had moved out of Diana Ross's pad to be reunited with his family, including mother and sisters who had relocated to the West Coast. The family moved into a substantial property on Queens Road and were able to enjoy the quintessential LA lifestyle. The family's new home was short-lived; their noisy rehearsals soon upset their more sedate neighbours, and Motown moved them to another, more secluded location in the shadow of the famous Hollywood Hills. The Jacksons' Tinsel Town dream was becoming a reality.

5

Big time

BIG TIME

The Jacksons had no time to rest on their laurels. Berry Gordy was anxious to repeat the boys' initial success with a strong follow-up single and album. Work began in earnest and the Corporation was commissioned to spin their magic yet again, the pressure was on. The result was a simple up-beat tune entitled *ABC*. It shared some of the same simple chord structures as *I Want You Back*, but had an even more infectious hook line. *ABC*, the title track from the forthcoming LP was written from scratch exclusively for the boys. The song was aimed fairly and squarely at the youth

BIG TIME

market. It epitomised what was referred to at the time as bubblegum pop, and was an exemplary example of that genre.

Released in February 1970, *ABC*, galloped to the top of the Billboard chart with just under 2.5 million sales. The Jacksons had the Midas touch. The Jackson Five brand was associated with lively wholesome music that transcended colour and age barriers — they were a marketing dream. In early Seventies America, popular music was still fairly segregated; the Jackson Five performed palatable, non-threatening, non-political tunes. Motown wanted to emphasise to the public at large that the group was the acceptable face of young black America.

It was time for the brothers to hit the road, to peddle their product and meet their adoring teenage fans. Nothing and no one had prepared the Jackson Five for what was about to confront them when they landed at Philadelphia International Airport, on 2 May 1970. The boys were greeted by thousands of screaming teenagers. Jackson mania had hit the Pennsylvania town in a big way. Police and security guards were out in force protecting the boys from over-eager wellwishers. Their limo needed a police escort for the journey to the

BIG TIME

Philadelphia Convention Centre, where the boys were due to perform. The Jackson Five's concert that night was barely audible to anyone in the auditorium, the screams drowned out the overworked sound system, but nobody seemed to care. Michael, only 11-years-old at the time was a bit traumatised by the experience; his older brothers were just amazed by the whole reception.

The month of May also saw the release of the band's third single, *The Love You Save*, it was another track to be lifted from the soon to be released *ABC* album. Spurred on, no doubt, by recent concert success and favourable headlines, it had little trouble making it to number one in the charts. True to his word Berry Gordy and his Motown Company had delivered the hat trick.

With no time to bask in their success, the Jackson Five released their much-anticipated second album, *ABC*. The second album was even more successful than the first. That summer the Jacksons would cause bedlam in their adopted town of Los Angeles, when they sang at the Forum. Berry Gordy was able to see first-hand the effect that his super group had on the audience. The fans rushed the stage overpowering security and forcing the brothers to be whisked away before

BIG TIME

they'd even completed the concert. These scenes were to be repeated across the US and eventually across the globe, as the boys fulfiled promotional and touring duties.

In August 1970 after releasing three successful dance numbers, the group put out their first ballad *I'll Be There*, Berry Gordy decided that the band should change their musical direction. He took personal charge of the project; it was a bit of a risk, as their audience fan base had already bought into the up-tempo feelgood tunes. Nevertheless Gordy was keen to expose the band's versatility, and secure their longevity. Gordy was proved right yet again when *I'll Be There* gave the boys their fourth consecutive US number one. This track would later appear on the Jackson Five's incredibly unimaginatively titled, *The Third Album*. One can only assume that Motown's creative department was having an off day.

The Jacksons continued a heavy toll of recording and live work, even managing to record the prerequisite Christmas offering for release later on in the year *Jackson Five, The Christmas Album*. This compilation of standard seasonal songs was given the somewhat less traditional Motown makeover. Christmas 1970 was a happy one in the Jackson household. They had managed a meteoric rise in a relatively short time and were reaping the rewards of their labour. Joe was happy with the way things were progressing, he had a great deal of respect for Berry Gordy and the way he was directing the Jacksons' career.

In January 1971 the Jacksons returned 'home' to Indiana for the first time since they'd hit the big time. Mayor Richard Hatcher was on the campaign trail again and invited the Jackson Five to play at West Side High School. The venue was packed and the Jackson Five did not disappoint the expectant audience. The local neighbourhood came out to greet them. That day the mayor awarded the boys the 'key to the city of Gary' in a ceremony at City Hall. Some of the very neighbours who had thought the Jacksons would never achieve anything added their voices to the welcome committee. On the front lawn of their old home someone had erected a placard: Welcome Home Jackson 5 Keepers Of The Dream. 2300 Jackson Street was even smaller than the boys remembered; they could hardly even remember how the property had accommodated them all. The group sped off in a limo, happy to be leaving the past behind them for a second time. Three decades

BIG TIME

would pass before Michael Jackson would return.

Mama's Pearl, an up-tempo tune, was released that month. Although another Corporation composition it failed to reach the top spot. Two months later *Never Can Say Goodbye*, hit the record shops, again it did not replicate the earlier chart success. The Jackson Five embarked on a national tour of concerts and public appearances, this helped to maintain their profile and record sales. The boys enjoyed life on the road, staying in five-star hotels and having room service. Owing to their popularity they were not really able to enjoy the outside world. Occasionally determined predominantly female fans would break through security cordons and enter the boys' rooms, to announce their undying love for one or all of the brothers. Michael's older brothers Jackie (19) Tito (17) were not fazed by these intermittent intrusions, but 12-year-old Michael felt more vulnerable by the constant attention. It was a very artificial environment for the boys, but they managed to entertain themselves with the usual pop star antics; pillow and water balloon fights. Michael would later remark that life on the road brought him closer to his brothers. The boys' education suffered from a lack of continuity.

BIG TIME

Although Michael did go to school, as his fame grew he needed private tuition.

In April 1971 the Jacksons finally bought a new spread in Encino California, approximately 25 miles from downtown Los Angeles at 4641 Hayvenhurst Ave. Set in a couple of acres, complete with accommodation for staff and that all-important almost Olympic-sized pool, it more than lived up to the superstar stereotype. Katherine Jackson insisted that they retain ownership of the 2300 Jackson Street property, in case their bubble were to burst. Katherine seemed to be the only member of the family that actually missed Gary, not so much the area, which was falling deeper into urban decay, but more the feeling of community. The new homestead did not afford her that neighbourly feel. Like most of the privately owned properties on Hayvenhurst, visitors to the Jacksons' residence were monitored on CCTV by security guards, before being allowed to enter via the imposing electronic gates. Their newly acquired wealth was also on display on the driveway. Joe indulged his passion for prestigious marques by splashing out on a Mercedes soft-top coupé, whilst Jackie lovingly waxed, and waxed lyrical about, his new Datsun 240z, one of the few Datsun models not suited to minicab work.

6

Jumping ship

I n September 1971, the Jacksons starred in their own television show – *Goin' Back to Indiana*. The special programme was broadcast at prime time by ABC and featured footage from their recent trip to Gary. The network was keen to cash in on the boys ever-growing popularity. The commissioning editor at ABC loved the idea that the boys hailed from a stable family unit, as well as their rags to riches fairytale.

Motown had cleverly 'labelled' each of the boys fairly early on in their careers so that they were seen as individuals. The brothers were not pigeonholed as rigidly as the Spice Girls, but Jackie

JUMPING SHIP

was definitely 'Sporty', he was an extremely talented athlete and in another life would most likely have become a highly successful professional basketball player. Tito liked to dabble with classic cars and anything mechanical. Marlon excelled at dancing, he would certainly give Michael a run for his money and choreographed lots of the band's moves. Jermaine was the eye-candy heartbreaker of the group conforming to many a teenage girl's fantasy, the ladies wanted him and the men wanted to be him. Michael, the star turn, enjoyed drawing pictures and keeping pets. The new house allowed him to realise his hobby, eventually accumulating a mini zoo.

With no drink, no drugs, no scandals, and with a fervently religious homemaker mother, the Jacksons had become America's premier family. It was this image that landed the Jacksons with their very own cartoon series – The Jackson 5ive. In their day before the music video 30-minute cartoons were considered as cool as the Simpsons. Michael and his brothers 'danced and sang' all of their hits, but their voices were recorded by actors. The Saturday morning cult series ran for 23 episodes from September 1971.

At the end of 1971, Motown decided to release

JUMPING SHIP

Michael Jackson's first solo effort. The song, *Got To Be There*, shared more than a passing resemblance to the Jackson Five's first ballad. With this 'familiar feel' factor, coupled with Motown's big orchestral sound, the tune was always guaranteed to become an instant classic though not a number one hit. Joe was weary of singling Michael out for special attention, and in the past had been annoyed when the band had been referred to as: "Michael Jackson and the Jackson Five". The novelty of the act was that it was a family business; everyone should get a piece of the action. Unfortunately for the Jacksons another ambitious singing family was emerging onto the scene. Enter the Osmonds. Cute, sweet and white, the Osmonds ticked even more boxes then the Jacksons on the 'marketable' form. The two families were evenly matched. The Jacksons were charming, the Osmonds were charming, the Jacksons were musicians, the Osmonds were musicians, the Jacksons could dance, and the Osmonds were charming. The Osmonds' middle-of-the-road pop music initially fared even better in the UK than the Jacksons' material.

The Jacksons were prolific artists with an extremely high work-rate; by the mid-Seventies

JUMPING SHIP

they had released in the region of 20 albums and produced 11 number ones, but had recorded approximately 500 songs. Motown had deemed it fit to only release about 40 per cent of their overall material. In addition they had toured worldwide covering everywhere from Africa to New Zealand. Joe and his sons were no longer satisfied by the way Motown was leading the group. By now Michael and his brothers were already old hands in the music industry, they were an established live act and had lots of studio time under their belt. Their growing confidence became more evident. Now no longer the new kids on the block, the Jackson Five wanted to have greater creative and commercial autonomy. They were not allowed to pen their own material thereby being denied any access to lucrative publishing copyrights. It is a grievance that has since been expressed by other major ex-Motown stars.

They found Motown's tight control on their careers exasperating. Motown dictated what the band released and how it would be marketed. Berry Gordy was concentrating on other aspects of his ever-expanding empire; he wanted to do for movies what he'd done for music. As a result Gordy resigned as President of Motown Records to be

JUMPING SHIP

succeeded by Ewart G Abner Jnr. Gordy still maintained overall control as Chairman of Motown Industries. Joe Jackson was desperate to break his boys out of their teeny-bopper image. Music trends were changing, and he didn't want them to be left behind. The sound of sweet bubblegum tunes was being replaced with that of electronic disco. The Jacksons released *Dancing Machine* in 1974. It was a funky mature album, which brought the band bang up to date. However the band as always was denied any creative input.

Joe took the group to Las Vegas, to prove that his boys could entertain mainstream older, more sophisticated audiences. The Jacksons' pilgrimage to the capital of gambling followed in the footsteps of Vegas veterans Sammy Davies Jnr, Elvis Presley and Frank Sinatra. The brothers performed a type of cabaret act, which included limited appearances by their sisters Janet and LaToya. Katherine was not overwhelmed with her family playing at these, albeit lavish 'dens of iniquity', but seeing all of her children (minus Rebbie) on stage together warmed her heart.

Despite their continuously successful live performances, be it in concert, on the Vegas stage, or on television, on vinyl they were stalling.

MICHAEL JACKSON

JUMPING SHIP

Records sales were at an all-time low, and morale at the Jackson camp was the same. Joe Jackson called a family meeting at the Hayvenhurst House. Jermaine was absent from proceedings, holidaying abroad with his wife at the time. Jermaine married Gordy's daughter Hazel, on 15 December 1973. Being married to the boss's daughter made the brothers wary of Jermaine's allegiances.

The Jackson Five were thankful to Berry Gordy – they admired and respected him, but they were starting to feel neglected. Michael has since stated that he saw him as a father figure. However the band decided things would have to change if they were to have any kind of credible future. So on that warm spring evening in 1975, the Jackson Five decided it was time to jump ship.

Joe Jackson approached CBS Records for a new deal. The new CBS President, Walter Yetnikoff, was initially sceptical. He felt that the band's heyday was well behind them, but he went to see them in Vegas nonetheless. It was Yetnikoff's first year in the job and he really wanted to sign a big act that would make a lasting impression. He saw Michael's superstar status straight away; though he was not quite as impressed with the group's material.

JUMPING SHIP

Yetnikoff offered the Jackson Five a favourable contract, and the band was happy to become part of the global CBS brand. Jermaine Jackson had divided loyalties; he had to make a choice between the Jackson Family and his new in-laws at Motown. Jermaine opted for Motown. This made things difficult for all concerned, the once tightly knit family was beginning to unravel. Berry Gordy had inferred that one day Jermaine could become head honcho at his 'family firm', the Jacksons put on a brave face but were desperately hurt by Jermaine's decision.

The band was in for another shock, they had relinquished their 'Jackson Five' name when they joined Motown. The record company had registered the name and there was absolutely nothing that the band could do about it. Their former employers also issued legal proceedings against the family for breaching their contract by bailing out early. The Jacksons counter-sued, the lawyers salivated, this was not going to be a cheap or amicable split. The whole business would eventually cost the Jacksons in excess of $2 million and six years to resolve.

Michael really wanted to write and produce his own material, Motown hadn't allowed him the freedom he craved and now it was time to redress

JUMPING SHIP

the balance. In 1976 he got his wishes, when the newly named Jacksons released their first self-titled album for CBS Records on their Epic Record Label, *The Jacksons*. The group were given the opportunity to contribute to and co-produce a couple of the tracks. CBS wanted to give the Jacksons the hard sell. The public had to know that the band were back with a new label and with a new product to push. They went on the road again, this time with Randy filling Jermaine's shoes. The boys' follow-up album, *Goin' Places* didn't really go anywhere in the charts, so by the time the third album was due, CBS were getting worried. This gave the Jacksons the opportunity to show their worth. The brothers were itching to be more hands-on. So when they were given a make-or-break chance to write and produce part of their third album, *Destiny*, they were delighted.

The *Destiny* LP marked the band's return to form, with classic disco tracks, *Shake Your Body (Down To The Ground)* and *Blame It On The Boogie*. Underpinned by a throbbing bass line both tunes allowed Michael to display his top end vocal range, and became instant floor-fillers on both sides of the Atlantic. True disco lovers around the world ensured that *Shake Your Body (Down To The Ground)* would eventually go platinum.

7

Flying solo

MICHAEL JACKSON

FLYING SOLO

With a little encouragement from his former mentor Diana Ross, Michael went up for the part of the scarecrow in Sidney Lumet's *The Wiz*. This was a remake of the 1939 MGM classic, *The Wizard of Oz* but featuring African-American artists. Diana Ross played Dorothy, whilst comedian Richard Pryor, was cast as the wizard. The Kansas countryside was swapped for the slightly more urban streets of Harlem, only Toto, that's Toto not Tito, remained unchanged. Michael stole the show, as he danced through the feature and sang *Ease on Down The Road*. At the time it was the most expensive musical ever made

FLYING SOLO

and was generally panned by the reviewers, but Michael Jackson put in a perfect performance and won critical acclaim.

Perhaps by way of compensation this was also the year that Michael Jackson purchased his first Rolls Royce, although he couldn't drive and it would be a few years before he got his license.

It was during the filming of *The Wiz* that Michael met legendary music composer and producer, Quincy Jones. Michael had been dying to do a solo album ever since he signed to CBS and he asked Jones if he could recommend a good producer, Jones willingly offered his own services. This was to be one of the most pivotal creative and business decisions that Jones and the 19-year-old would ever make. Songwriters made hundreds of submissions from which Jackson and Jones selected their top tunes. Jones recruited Rod Temperton who was a keyboard player and composer for a British soul band called Heatwave.

Temperton, possibly Cleethorpes best-ever export, penned the title track of the new album *Off The Wall*. However it was the timeless much sampled melodic *Rock With You* that would get to number one and prove to be one of Temperton's finest hours, well three minutes and 40 seconds to be precise. The northern seaside-resort songwriter also has Michael Macdonald's *Sweet Freedom* as well as tracks for Aretha Franklin and George Benson on his extensive CV. Jones was constantly impressed with Michael's preparation. Michael tackled his recording sessions with military precision; with a thorough Motown training behind him he was fully cognisant of studio costs and always turned up fully prepared to get down to business.

For the cover of new album Michael posed against a red brick wall whilst wearing black tie and his trademark glowing white socks. It was a new-look confident adult Michael Jackson that had emerged. The album spawned two US number one singles, *Rock With You* and *Don't Stop 'Til You Get Enough* and sold nearly 20 million worldwide. Michael was disappointed when *Off The Wall* only obtained one Grammy, he was adamant that his next effort would be even more successful.

Shortly after this an event that was to deeply traumatise the family occurred; but it also brought them closer together. Randy was involved in a near-fatal car crash. After sustaining multiple injuries to his legs, the family was informed that he might have to undergo amputation. Luckily

FLYING SOLO

with intensive treatment and his family's support Randy made almost a full recovery in under a year.

Michael had to fulfil recording and concert duties with his brothers, for the *Triumph* LP, before he could embark on his own follow-up album. Michael was a strong believer in family commitments but also wanted to break away and do his own thing long-term. He felt pressures from his mother, father and brothers, who all relied on him for their communal success. Michael approached top entertainment lawyer John Branca to renegotiate a new contact for him with Walter Yetnikoff. Branca had gone from high school drop-out to high-flying legal eagle building up an impressive rock n' roll client portfolio which included The Beach Boys, Rolling Stones and The Doors. The new deal gave Michael a bigger share of royalties, but also it ensured that his brothers would not be dropped even if he were no longer part of The Jacksons.

8

Making his mark

MICHAEL JACKSON

MAKING HIS MARK

B y the summer of 1982 Michael Jackson couldn't wait to get back into the studio with friend and producer Quincy Jones. It had been three years since *Off The Wall* had hit the streets and Michael was restless. Things were different by now in the Jackson household, most of the siblings had flown the nest. Only, LaToya, Michael, Randy and Janet remained. Michael was spending a lot of time at the house; increased fame meant that fans regularly congregated outside the property. It was reported that once an entire family broke into the house and started wondering round enjoying their private tour. The fame that Michael had acquired seemed to make him something of a prisoner in his own home.

Jackson and Jones again called upon the talents of Temperton for the second album. They had an initial production budget of about half-a-million dollars. As was the system at the time, potential songwriters were approached via their agents and given the chance to pitch ideas. When word got out that Jackson was working on a new album (originally titled *Starlight*), the Epic Record Label was inundated with unsolicited commissions. Jones planned the pace and feel of the album, trying to ensure their final product would have a good mixture and mood.

With his eye firmly fixed on broad appeal Jackson enlisted the help of highly respected rock guitarist Edward Van Halen for *Beat It*. Commercially this made sure that the single would attain some credibility in the rock community. Using high-profile guitarists was a trick Michael would use again — Slash, Steve Stevens and Carlos Santana would all pop up on future Jackson projects. Another high-profile collaboration was Michael's duet with Paul McCartney on the saccharine first single release, *The Girl is Mine*.

MICHAEL JACKSON

MAKING HIS MARK

In addition to composing, *Lady In My Life*, Temperton came up with the title track, *Thriller*, and the monster was born. *Thriller* the single and then the John Landis video that accompanied it took on a momentum of its own. The mini-movie depicted Michael on an innocent date with a young girlfriend then things turn sour and he transforms into a werewolf, before dancing off with his zombie mates. The late, great Vincent Price provided a hammy horror rap. Jackson approached Landis to direct the video having been a fan of his cult caper *An American Werewolf in London*. Michael was so enthusiastic about the project that wanted to splash out in the region of $600,000 on it. In those days it was unheard of to spend such a vast amount of money on a pop video. However, Jackson got his way and the production was eventually financed through shrewd distribution deals brokered by Branca.

Michael's on-screen sweetheart was played by actress and ex-*Playboy* Playmate, Ola Ray. She had previously appeared in *48 Hours* and subsequently turned up with Eddie Murphy in *Beverly Hills Cop II*. MTV premiered the video on 2 December 1983; the hype surrounding it went into overdrive. The anticipation both in and outside the industry was tangible; the 14-minute promo film set new standards for pop music videos.

Even the film about the making of the *Thriller* video, released nearly a year after the first single, became an unprecedented best-seller. The 'making of' documentary was produced as a way of recouping costs that had spiralled out of control in the original video. The bandwagon was rolling and nothing could stop it. Six singles were eventually released and each newly released track only served to promote the album sales even more, it was a vicious, highly lucrative circle. It became the must-have record in everyone's collection. Even when it seemed as though everyone in the world had a copy, *Thriller* would sell even more. At its height there was what could only be described as a feeding frenzy as almost 500,000 copies a week went flying off the shelves.

The Guinness Book of Records declared the album the biggest-selling of all time after achieving worldwide sales of 25 million, but the album would go on to sell in excess of 50 million.

Motown were partly responsible for the cataclysmic success of *Thriller*. In March 1983 Motown celebrated its 25th anniversary. The extremely tenacious Suzanne De Passe, who eventually rose through the ranks to become President of Motown Records, was busy trying to organise acts

MAKING HIS MARK

for the television extravaganza. Owing to various strained relationships between Motown and some of their ex-artists, not her own management skills, this was proving to be a very difficult task. She needed to employ all of her powers of persuasion to secure acts. Motown was no longer the force that it had been. Diana Ross who had by now left the label would not commit to being reunited with the Supremes. Other classic acts such as the The Temptations and Marvin Gaye had also flown the nest, and the Jacksons separation from the company still left a sour taste with the family. However business is business, Joe Jackson saw the benefits of the high-profile exposure and Epic Records had no objections with their artists celebrating Motown's anniversary.

Michael was less convinced. He really didn't need the publicity at the time, *Thriller* had only recently been released and the tills were still ringing loudly. Berry Gordy approached Michael personally, although they had had a less than amicable split, the two men still maintained a great deal of respect for one another. In fact they had a lot in common. Each knew exactly what they wanted and were prepared to work extremely hard.

Although reluctant to take part, Michael

agreed to perform with his brothers as long as he could do his current single, *Billie Jean*. On 25 March, a Friday night, The Jacksons reunited with Jermaine to perform a medley of their Motown hits. After the set Michael remained behind on stage, it had been his first live performance since the release of *Thriller*. People who had forgotten him were suddenly about to be reminded of his abilities. As the distinctive bass line kicked in he began to make his moves, donning a black fedora and sporting the rhinestone glove Jackson span, posed and moonwalked his way into contemporary folk law. The audience were spellbound, they knew that they were experiencing something very special that evening. Jackson's dance routine encompassed a lifetime of dancers and performers, from Fred Astaire, Sammy Davies Jnr and James Brown to the LA street scene. It covered more than the 25 years that Motown were celebrating. Michael received a standing ovation. Berry Gordy was one of the most vocal to sing his praise. As his brothers greeted him in the wings they were all pumped-up. This was partly as a result of their pride and admiration and partly because they knew that his success and performance could rub off on them.

Ever the perfectionist, instead of being elated

by his performance, Jackson was in tears. He was upset because he didn't think that his performance was up to his own expectations.

After the Motown 25th Anniversary, which was broadcast on the ABC Network and eventually worldwide, *Thriller* record sells received another boost. The following week, although Michael had not recorded on the Motown Label for nearly 10 years, their offices were bombarded with fan mail, no doubt to the consternation of Epic Records.

9

Beyond celebrity

*Michael Jackson (second right) performing with his brothers
in The Jackson Five. 'I want you back' on Motown went to the
number one spot in the Billboard chart in January 1970.
Their next two singles, 'ABC' and 'The Love you Save' also went
straight to number one, making it a hat trick for the boys.
From left to right: Tito, Marlon, Jackie, Michael and Jermaine*

The ground-breaking video for Michael's single 'Thriller' – directed by John Landis, was premiered on MTV on 2 December 1983. The 14-minute promo film set new standards for pop music videos. The single sold in excess of 25 million copies.

Michael Jackson at Wembley Stadium on his BAD world tour (1987 – 1989). His dance moves and outfits are as much a part of his live shows as his music. He is the consummate showman leaving fans awe-inspired by his performances.

Michael Jackson provokes a reaction like no other. He has sung and danced his way in to the record books during the past four decades, and still remains one of the most famous people on the planet.

BEYOND CELEBRITY

More than 12 months later, the *Thriller* hype showed little sign of abating. In January 1984 Michael narrowly escaped serious injury when he was shooting a commercial for Pepsi Cola. He was about to perform a specially adapted version of *Billie Jean* for the soft-drink manu-facturer. His hair was set ablaze by the pyrotechnics. At the time there was panic all round. Nobody knew how badly hurt he was. News crews captured the moment that he was stretchered off into an ambulance; Jackson's distinctive gloved hand waved tentatively.

BEYOND CELEBRITY

Thankfully Michael's injuries were not life-threatening or disfiguring. He received second- and third-degree burns to the side of his head and the back of his hand. The hair was to grow back and no permanent damage was sustained. This was the second on-stage injury to hospitalise Jackson. Prior to the release *Off The Wall*, Jackson tripped during a dance rehearsal and broken his nose. As a result he underwent rhinoplasty.

The Pepsi ad campaign was a lucrative one and the incident only served to increase Jackson's publicity and pump up the sales of 'that' album. Though not accepting liability, the soft drinks company paid the star $1.5 million dollars in compensation. Michael donated the money to a Californian burns unit to benefit other victims. It was much later, whilst he was visiting the unit that he was photographed inside a hyperbaric chamber – a piece of equipment used in the treatment of burns victims. This picture was to be the foundations for the tabloid headlines that speculated that Jackson wanted to prevent ageing and, as a result, slept in this contraption. It didn't take long before the rumour and the picture had circulated the globe. The stories didn't actually hurt Jackson's appeal at all, they only seemed to fuel further speculation and interest.

MICHAEL JACKSON

BEYOND CELEBRITY

Michael put the events of the last month firmly behind him, and on 28 February 1984 he attended the much-anticipated 26th Annual Grammy Award Ceremony – one of the music industry's most prestigious events. Everyone knew that it was going to be Jackson's night, but no one was sure how many Grammies he would moonwalk away with. Actress Brooke Shields escorted Jackson to the event. The couple had similar backgrounds. Brooke Shields, like Jackson, had been a child star. They were both religious, Jackson a Jehovah Witness, Shields a Roman Catholic. Her mother manager had Brooke modelling from the age of 11 months. The 19-year-old's major claim to fame was a co-starring role in the exotic 1980-remake of *The Blue Lagoon* and a Calvin Kline Jeans endorsement. All of this led to the Princeton graduate being dubbed 'The Face Of The Eighties' by US *Time Magazine*. In recent years she has become more famous for being the ex-Mrs Andre Agassi and her ill-fated Channel 4 screened sitcom *Suddenly Susan*. Brooke Shields continued to date Michael Jackson on and off for about a decade, but she wasn't the first star with whom Michael was romantically linked. Michael's first girlfriend was Tatum Beatrice O'Neal and she

BEYOND CELEBRITY

had the distinction of being the youngest-ever actor to win an Oscar for Best Supporting Actress, opposite her father, Ryan, in *Paper Moon*. The Hollywood wild-child went onto to become the ex-Mrs John MacEnroe. New balls, please.

The star-studded 1984 Grammy's ceremony, hosted by caustic comedienne Joan Rivers, was a glittering event. That night Jackson won an unprecedented, record breaking eight Grammies including: Record Of The Year for *Beat It*, Album Of The Year for *Thriller*, Best R'n'B and Blues for *Billie Jean* and Best Male Vocal Performance. During one of his acceptance speeches, Jackson paid a moving tribute to fellow Motown legend Jackie Wilson, who had died a month earlier at the age of 49 after being semi-comatose for the last eight years. He went on to collect another Grammy for *The Making of Thriller* video the following year making the final toll nine Grammies for one album.

So now it was official, Michael Jackson was the most famous entertainer in the known universe. In the space of five years his status had risen from celebrity, to A-list celebrity, to beyond celebrity. Jackson's fame was stratospheric. He was constantly photographed, other celebrities wanted to be seen with him and major commercial brands wanted to be associated with him. It wasn't only his status that had changed in a short period of time, his physical appearance had altered also. He had lost weight; he'd had a nose job, and his trademark Afro had been 'replaced' with permed hair. In addition and most alarmingly, his skin colour had changed. It was becoming lighter. Shortly after Jackson had finished recording the *Thriller* album he noticed blotchy patches appearing on his face and body. Jackson is one of millions who suffers from vitiligo. This skin condition causes 'spontaneous irregular depigmentation' for its sufferers. It is neither painful nor contagious but there is no known cure for the illness that can be dramatic, especially in dark-skinned peoples.

Vitiligo was prevalent on Joe Jackson's side of the family. It can develop at any stage of life. In an effort to even out his skin tone, Michael routinely uses make-up on his face and hands. Michael was robust in reputing allegations of wanting to be white and when, some years later, he was interviewed by Oprah Winfrey, he stated: "I'm a black American, I am proud to be a black American, I am proud of my race I am proud of who I am. I have a lot of pride and dignity."

Michael and his brothers were back on the road

BEYOND CELEBRITY

again in the summer of 1984 with their *Victory* tour. Michael was a reluctant recruit and it was to be the last time that he would ever tour with The Jacksons. Michael wanted to pursue personal projects, but his mother Katherine persuaded him otherwise. Michael reportedly wanted the tour to the called 'The Final Curtain Tour' in an effort to drive the message home.

It was a gruelling schedule which took six months to complete, and took its toll on Michael. It was the most extravagant stage show that the brothers had ever endeavoured. Michael was already displaying an interest in the visual tricks that would play such a major part in his own future solo concerts. Understandably the crowds were really attending to see superstar Michael Jackson as opposed to the Jackson Brothers. He was stealing the limelight. It was becoming increasingly obvious that his brothers could no longer credibly 'share' the stage with Michael. In the public's eyes they seemed to be relegated to his backing band. In truth it was difficult for anyone else to hold the audience's attention when he was around. His brothers found it strange and difficult to view Michael as a superstar, to them he's always been their little brother Mike. The Jacksons' album *Victory* which the latest tour was promoting, didn't do particularly well in the charts, but the concerts set a new world record for attendance. Each of the brothers is thought to have walked away with about $5 million from the tour; Michael donated his share to charity.

Prior to the concerts Michael got himself a new personal manager. Joe Jackson had managed him and his brothers for most of their lives, but Michael felt that it was now time for a change. Frank M Dileo was the man charged with moving Michael Jackson's career forward. A daunting task that the larger-than-life Dileo (nicknamed 'Tookie') relished. Pittsburgh-born Dileo was a tough-talking, cigar-chewing, heftily built five-foot-three-inch maverick. Dileo looked like a 'wise guy' and in fact he went on to appear in Scorsese's 1990 mobster masterpiece *Goodfellas*.

Dileo landed his role with Jackson after achieving great success with Cyndi Lauper and Meatloaf among other acts. He had proved his worth as a supreme publicist at Epic Records and gained a reputation as a man who gets the job done. Jackson and Dileo made an odd couple as they went about their business together. Michael with his slender five-foot-ten frame was almost as tall as Dileo was wide, they were the 'little and large' of the pop

BEYOND CELEBRITY

music industry. On the personality front they also complemented one another. Michael's softly spoken coy persona was the perfect antidote to Frank's brassy, bold, 'blinging' style.

During the long-haul *Victory* tour, Jackson, Dileo and Branca secured one of the shrewdest business deals in the history of music publishing. Michael's interest in obtaining publishing rights may have been initially ignited after a conversation he had with Sir Paul McCartney. The two respected artists collaborated on *The Girl is Mine* and later on *Say, Say, Say*. There had been a recent trend for many advertising campaigns to feature long-forgotten tracks from yesteryear. One of the reasons the Jacksons had left Motown was because they were being denied any publishing rights. In the autumn of 1984 Michael paid just under $50 million for ATV Music Publishing House. This company owned the rights to many classic songs including scores of Lennon and McCartney, or should that be McCartney and Lennon's penned compositions including *Yesterday*, *Hey Jude* and *All You Need Is Love*. It spanned seven years of the groups' historic tenure. There were also classics by other artists including Little Richard's *Tutti Fruitti* and Elvis's *Love Me Tender*.

A few years earlier McCartney was given the

option of purchasing the rights to these songs, but after negotiations with Lennon's widow Yoko Ono broke down, he lost the opportunity. McCartney had hoped that Ono would put up half of the cash, but she got cold feet. As the new owner, Jackson would now have complete control of McCartney's old Beatles' material, and could dictate when and where it was used. Over the years this acquisition has earned Michael a not so small fortune – the stock was valued at $450 million (November 2003).

Over on this side of the pond in 1984, ex-Boomtown Rats' frontman Sir Bob Geldof witnessed Michael Burke's heart-wrenching famine report from Ethiopia. Everyone who viewed the memorable BBC footage was moved by it, but it was Geldof who decided that he must do something about it. He collaborated with Midge Ure of Ultravox fame on a charity single *Do They Know It's Christmas*. Together they persuaded the cream of the pop music industry to donate their services. Among those who turned up one Sunday morning at the London recording studio included Duran Duran, David Bowie, Paul McCartney, Sting and U2.

The Band Aid single inspired US film star Harry Belafonte to set up a similar scheme. Lionel Richie became involved in the project and brought

BEYOND CELEBRITY

Stevie Wonder and Michael Jackson on board. With Quincy Jones at the production helm, Jackson and Richie wrote *We Are The World*. Like their British counterparts the team then recruited the best and biggest names of US talent to perform the song. As with the UK artists, the American performers left their egos at the studio door and mucked in for the cause. Among the 45 American artists who took part in yet another historic recording were Diana Ross, Tina Turner, Bruce Springsteen and Bette Midler. The 1985 US single topped the charts on both sides of the water and both singles helped to raise $60 million in aid for Africa. The subsequent Live Aid Concerts went on to put another estimated $200 million into the coffers.

Not only CBS and his fans, but also the entertainment industry as a whole was waiting for Michael Jackson to produce a follow-up to *Thriller*. The pressure to top that album was immense. Financially the *Thriller* project including the LP, video, the making of the video, royalties and other related marketing added well over $100 million to Michael's bank balance. As well as boosting Michael's popularity, *Thriller* had an added spin-off effect. The success of that record somehow increased the sale of other non-related records. The

MICHAEL JACKSON

BEYOND CELEBRITY

US music industry had been experiencing a slump in the early Eighties, but the record-buying public seemed to get the bug back with the release of *Thriller*. It's hard to believe now, but at the time the album had such an effect on the entertainment economy that even Wall Street stockbrokers were eagerly anticipating a new solo release. But Michael had other things on his mind.

Michael had been a life-long fan of Walt Disney as well as a regular visitor to Disneyland in California. So he was delighted to become a Disney attraction, when he starred in the specially commissioned *Captain EO* movie. Disney had originally approached Jackson to come up with an idea for a new ride. Michael developed storylines with George Lucas at his vast Skywalker Ranch. Michael ended up co-writing and starring in the title role alongside Angelica Houston. He also composed a couple of songs for the movie. Although George Lucas produced and Francis Ford Coppola directed the movie, it lasted just 17 minutes, but took over a year to make at a cost of over $25 million. The 3D film was crammed full of special effects, and screened in Disney cinemas.

10

It's not all bad

MICHAEL JACKSON

IT'S NOT ALL BAD

Michael Jackson's follow-up album to *Thriller – Bad –* finally saw the light of day in the summer of 1987. Michael had taken on the mammoth task of writing eight of the 10 songs. Quincy Jones was again in charge of production. Yetnikoff and CBS were determined to make the launch of the new album an epic event. US Radio stations ran promotional competitions giving away hundreds of copies of *Bad*, and TV stations screened documentaries about Jackson to whet the public's appetite. The rocky up-tempo title track revealed a harder edge to Jackson, the $2-million-accompanying video, directed by Martin Scorsese was shot in a

IT'S NOT ALL BAD

Harlem subway. Clad in a black outfit displaying punk-like belts, buckles and zips; it was a *West Side Story* spoof of the New York gangland scene.

The first track to be released was *I Just Can't Stop Loving You* which reached the number one spot. It was a duet that Michael performed with Siedah Garret who had previously worked with the Commodores and Chaka Khan. Together with Glen Ballard, she wrote the second number one of the album *Man In The Mirror* which was an uplifting spiritual tune featuring gospel singers, The Winans and The Andrea Crouch Choir. Jackson went on to donate all the royalties from the single to an LA charity for the terminally ill. Meanwhile Siedah Garret went on tour with Michael Jackson, and then a few years later, she came over to Britain and headed up the London-based, acid jazz outfit, the Brand New Heavies. Michael also partnered fellow ex-Motown star Stevie Wonder in a duet track called *Just Good Friends* which was never released as a single.

The album was not as critically acclaimed as *Thriller* but UK fans welcomed it enthusiastically, keeping it in the charts for over 100 weeks. According to the record company, the British public gorged themselves on 150,000 copies of the

IT'S NOT ALL BAD

new album in one day. The album gave Jackson five US number ones, and six top ten singles in Britain. Though not as successful as *Thriller*, it did shift nearly 30 million copies to become the second biggest selling (non-soundtrack) album of all time. With *Thriller* having smashed all records and setting such unrealistic expectations, its hardly surprising that *Bad* did not fare as well.

Once again Michael Jackson took to the road to pump his latest product. The first stop on his mega-Pepsi-sponsored *Bad* world tour was the Korakuen Stadium in Tokyo. He played 14 sell-out shows at the venue. During the 16 months the band crossed four continents, visited 15 countries and broke stadium records as they went. The 150-strong cast and crew trundled into towns around the globe. Two dates at Rome's Flaminio Stadium kicked off the European leg of the tour. When Jackson's show touched down in London for a seven-night residency at Wembley, Michael stayed at Park Lane's opulent Dorchester Hotel in the £2,000 per night Oliver Mussel Suite. Jackson's personal entourage occupied an entire floor or two. Over 500,000 punters packed into Wembley during the week-long run, setting a new record for the north London stadium.

MICHAEL JACKSON

IT'S NOT ALL BAD

Kim Wilde was one of the support acts to perform in front of a packed Wembley Stadium. She met Michael briefly and he introduced her to Bubbles his chimp. The monkey had been acquired two years earlier from a cancer research laboratory where the animal faced an uncertain future. Bubbles lived at Michael's mini-home-zoo at Hayvenhurst, but gained semi-celebrity status when Michael took him out in public. There was even a cuddly toy version of Bubbles manufactured in the early Nineties. Bubbles has since retired to an animal sanctuary.

Michael's *Bad* show had been partly designed by Las Vegas big cat magicians Siegfried and Roy (Siegfried Fischbacher and Roy Horn). Prior to Roy being severely mauled by Montecore, a 600-pound white Bengal tiger in October 2003, the entertainers were Vegas's most popular illusionist act. Their career has spanned 35 years, and they coined the tagline 'Masters of the Impossible'. Michael, a long-time fan, approached the daring German duo to be consultants for his concerts. In return he agreed to write an opening tune for their MGM Mirage Hotel shows.

Anyone who has seen Jackson live will appreciate that the event is more a theatrical, stage show musical than a 'straight' concert. He interprets his songs using various set-piece scenarios. His dance moves are as important as his vocals. The occasion is deliberately orchestrated so that the audiences witness a true spectacle. Even the most cynical of viewers soon gets wrapped up in the hype. Two giant video screens display images of Jackson through the years; as he grows and metamorphosises in front of your eyes, the atmosphere gradually reaches a crescendo so that before long the audience is cheering those recorded images, long before glimpsing the artist. Then after the support acts and a suitable pause, a bank of high voltage lights rise from the stage into the rafters. As the lights, smoke and deafening din settles, Michael Jackson is revealed as though deposited from another planet.

Michael likes to make a big entrance. Later in 1992, his *Dangerous* tour opened with Michael being launched 10 feet into the air and on to the stage via a trapdoor as a hail of pyrotechnics rain down behind him. Magician David Copperfield designed the box of tricks for this tour. Jackson's exit was no less dramatic; it entailed 'Michael' having a jetpack strapped to his back and being wished 'Godspeed' as he flies off into the night.

MICHAEL JACKSON

IT'S NOT ALL BAD

Despite being taken through a range of emotions during the two-hour show, it's the one time that the audience are left truly speechless.

Just before the stunt Jackson, wearing a crash helmet, changes places with a stunt pilot. The real Michael Jackson makes a much less glamourous low-profile exit from the stage, being wheeled off whilst crouched down in a crate. It's hardly surprising that Michael Jackson was not allowed to operate the hydrogen peroxide powered 'Rocketbelt' with its 320lbs of thrust, but the illusion works brilliantly nonetheless.

When the *Bad* roadshow parked up in Madison Square Gardens, Michael donated a $600,000 cheque to the United Negro College. The educational charity funds underprivileged but able black students who want to go to university. Throughout the tour the Jackson team also invited sick children to see the superstar, they were given the full VIP treatment. Jackson would also make a point of visiting various establishments from hospitals to orphanages. Much of the work that Jackson did off-stage went unreported.

In addition to breaking attendance records, the concerts were seen by over 4 million people. The *Bad* tour set new records for pop profits. It is the

IT'S NOT ALL BAD

highest grossing tour in history, netting a whopping $125 million. At the end of the tour Frank Dileo parted company with Michael Jackson, their five-year partnership coming to an end. Sandy Gallin went on to fill his shoes.

11

Down time

DOWN TIME

While Jackson was on tour he did occasionally return to the US on house-hunting expeditions. Michael felt that he had outgrown Hayvenhurst and wanted the freedom that his own place would afford him. Although a first-time buyer, Jackson was not faced with the usual mortgage problems, so he opted to forgo the regular three-bed semi, in lieu of something more palatial. In early 1988 Jackson completed on a 2,700-acre ranch called Sycamore. Paul McCartney had invited Jackson to the property when he was renting it out a few years earlier whilst filming the *Say Say, Say* video. John

DOWN TIME

Branca negotiated the deal with the then-owner, property developer William Bone for a knockdown price – a reputed $17 million.

Michael loved his property and immediately set about customising it to suit his personal tastes. The new owner started by changing its name. From now on his homestead: 5225, Figueroa Mountain Road would be known as Neverland Valley Ranch. The name was taken from the *Peter Pan* fairytale as Michael had always related to J M Barrie's little boy who wouldn't grow up. The ranch, situated approximately 100 miles north of LA in Santa Ynez Valley, gave Michael the space and freedom he yearned. Not quite 'Stella Street' but his neighbours include the Reagans, Bo Derek and action-hero, Steven Seagal. The nearest town is a small village called Los Olivos so the Neverland Ranch is the one of the main employers in the area.

The property, set in beautifully landscaped grounds cannot be seen from the road. A high fence and walls shield it and large, wrought iron gold-crest gates, greet visitors to the residence. There is a blue Neverland neon sign above the gates that is illuminated at night. A long driveway leads to the main house. There are over 20 separate buildings

DOWN TIME

in the complex, some of which house staff and guests. Michael generally sweeps around his grounds in golf buggies. Jackson's pad is decorated with ornate pieces of furniture – some antique, some not. There are many paintings adorning the walls that reflect the singer's interest in Greek mythology. Porcelain figurines are also dotted around Michael's personal space. This contrasts starkly with another of Jackson's passions. He is a self-confessed gadget freak, loving cutting edge, up-to-the-minute technology. Michael can spend hours on end playing with state-of-the-art video games in his home and has a specially constructed arcade.

Jackson is a fervent shopper who can sweep through his favourite stores like a whirlwind. Store managers often have difficulty keeping up with him as new *objects d'art* catch his eye. The singing star has been known to spend tens of thousands of dollars in less than an hour. At times Jackson's shopping sprees put even Elton John's expeditions to shame. Michael also enjoys buying toys, which he often distributes to children's hospitals.

At the heart of the sumptuous grounds there is a funfair, complete with Ferris wheel, bumper cars and a waltzer. A red and white canopy covers

DOWN TIME

a very traditional carousel next to the large swings. There's also a go-kart track and a miniature steam railway. The track circumnavigates the estate passing over bridges and alongside the man-made Lake Neverland. Passengers can board at the Flamingo Island Station and take the short journey to the Zoo Station where the tropical birds, elephants, giraffes and orang-utans are housed. It is now that one begins to realise that Neverland really is another world. Michael also enjoys the use of his own 100-seat private cinema – the space is large enough to accommodate hospital beds. Michael often invites sick children to his home, some of them are terminally ill and bed-ridden.

It was within this picturesque setting that Michael's friend, Hollywood screen-legend Elizabeth Francis Taylor wed her eighth husband, 39-year-old builder, Larry Fortensky. They met in a rehabilitation clinic and struck up a special bond. On the wedding day, Sunday, 6 October 1991, security was on high alert at the ranch. The paparazzi circled in helicopters during the ceremony trying to snatch a picture. One dare-devil photographer even managed to sky-dive into the proceedings in an effort to secure some highly sought-after snaps. Unfortunately, the

DOWN TIME

couple separated by 20 years, were to separate for good six years later.

Other less famous guests regularly turn up at Neverland when Michael throws open the gates and welcomes sick and underprivileged youngsters. They are given free run of the place, which never fails to impress children and adults alike. It always makes for a special occasion. Michael feels at home with children, he relishes their innocence and they appreciate his childlike qualities. The natural-born entertainer would often indulge them in food and water balloon fights, which he thoroughly enjoys and sometimes instigates.

The star also relishes the tranquillity that Neverland affords him. One of his favourite pastimes is climbing trees. He often climbs a particular tree, the 'Giving Tree' for inspiration. Michael has even composed songs there whilst sat amongst its branches: *Black or White* was conceived there amongst other tracks. Jackson also spends hours alone at his in-house recording studio. Although not commonly known, Jackson is a competent musician who plays a number of instruments (though not publicly) including drums, guitar and keyboards, but he does not write or read music. His writing process tends to begin with a

DOWN TIME

tune or a phrase going around his head, which he will then develop into a fully blown pop song.

In 1988 Michael Jackson released his long awaited autobiography, *Moonwalk*. Jackie Onassis edited the book. She mooted the idea of a Jackson book many years earlier, but he had been busy with other projects. Michael very much admired the former first lady and asked her advice on how to deal with the fame game. In his 283-page book, which he dedicated to dance hero Fred Astaire, he challenged the way the media portrayed him. In addition to telling his story, he tried to address the various rumours and speculation that had surrounded him. The publicity and curiosity surrounding Jackson ensured that the book became an instant best-seller.

The same year Michael Jackson released a fantasy musical feature film, *Moonwalker*. Directed by Jim Blashfield and Colin Chivers it featured live concert footage and fantasy sequences. Joe Pesci and Sean Lennon also put in an appearance. Very much aimed at the Jackson fan base, though not critically acclaimed, it did well on the video market, bringing home in the region of $30 million.

12

Not just black or white

MICHAEL JACKSON

NOT JUST BLACK OR WHITE

A fter nearly a year of intense negotiations, Sony Music (the parent company of CBS) brokered a new deal with Michael Jackson. It is the most lucrative golden handshake in the history of entertainment. He was given an initial six-album-deal and approximately $50 million as an incentive. Jackson was also given his own record label, MJJ. During this time he was working on tracks for his new album, *Dangerous*. Sony Music agreed the monumental contract hoping that Jackson would repeat the earlier successes of *Thriller* and *Bad*. The singer was committed to Sony for 15 years in total and the eventual

NOT JUST BLACK OR WHITE

package would land him $890 million.

Quincy Jones was absent from the latest Jackson production. Instead Michael turned to cutting-edge producers, Teddy Riley, Bill Bottrell and Bruce Swedien. Michael asked former *Thriller* video director, John Landis to work his magic again. The power of the visual medium dictated that a music video had to be released before the actual album. *Black or White* was the single and Sony wanted to pull out all the stops to promote it. The video featured the then 12-year-old actor, Macauley Culkin star of the *Home Alone* movies. Culkin starred alongside *Cheers* actor, George 'Norm' Wendt in the Jackson project. Following the filming Jackson and Culkin became firm friends. The video promoted racial harmony but also featured Michael Jackson smashing up a car and transforming into a panther. An estimated global audience of 500 million viewed the premiere.

The video made headlines because during the 11-minute film Jackson grabs his crotch no less than 13 times. The controversy created even more publicity for the album release a fortnight later. Jackson turned to Boyz N the Hood director John Singleton for his swing-beat single release, *Remember The Time*. The video featured comedy

NOT JUST BLACK OR WHITE

actor Eddie Murphy and Mrs David Bowie, Iman. In the video Michael shared his first screen kiss with the Somalian supermodel. Some years after working with Michael, Singleton would work his magic with another family member as he wrote and directed *Poetic Justice* starring Janet Jackson.

Dangerous, the album, sold well, shifting almost 30 million copies and stayed in the UK charts for nearly 100 weeks. *Black or White* was the only single to make it to number one on both sides of the Atlantic. Michael rehearsed with his band at Neverland Ranch in preparation for his *Dangerous* world tour. They started the series of concerts in June 1992. The first gig on the 69 date campaign was in Germany. They bedazzled the 75,000-strong audience, with tunes that spanned the decades from *I'll Be There* to *Black or White*. It was a full on multi-million dollar production. The set, which included a 270-foot stage, took three days to rig. Later that year, Michael's management sold the concert recording rights to US channel HBO. This entitled HBO to record the last show that Michael performed in Bucharest. For the privilege Michael Jackson netted $18 million. Michael Jackson also launched his Heal The World Foundation. It focused on helping young children

NOT JUST BLACK OR WHITE

in underprivileged communities around the world. The charity provided funds for other organisations that were specialists in the field, such as famine relief, education and health care.

At the beginning of 1993 Michael performed a medley of his hits, including *Billie Jean* and *Black or White* at Superbowl XXVII in Pasadena. One-hundred-and-thirty million viewers worldwide watched the highly sought after, half-time spot and there wasn't even an exposed nipple in sight.

On 10 February 1993, US chat show star Oprah Winfrey conducted a live interview with the entertainer at his Neverland home. For most viewers, and there were 90 million, this was the first time that they had seen inside the star's private magic kingdom. It was the most-watched TV interview ever, and the fourth most viewed programme in history. Jackson took Winfrey on a night-time grand tour of his house and fun fair. Winfrey was at liberty to ask him about any aspect of his professional or personal life. Michael revealed the extent of his plastic surgery, his skin condition and the traumatic childhood he had at the hands of his father Joe. He also used the opportunity to dispel any rumours that had been floating around. This was the first television interview that Jackson had given in a decade and it proved to be a PR coup. Jackson wanted to lose his elusive image. The public's response was to buy even more copies of the *Dangerous* album. Elizabeth Taylor even dropped by to talk about her friendship with the singer.

In March Michael and Brooke Shields attended the 35th Grammy Award Ceremony. That evening Janet Jackson presented her big brother with the Legend Award for "ongoing contributions to the recording industry". Barbra Streisand was the previous year's recipient and other past winners include Andrew Lloyd Webber, Liza Minnelli, Smokey Robinson and Aretha Franklin.

That summer Michael continued with the next leg of his lengthy *Dangerous* world tour in Thailand. Then in August 1993 the LAPD received an accusation of alleged child molestation levelled against Michael Jackson, which would rock his world. It did not take long for the information to leak to the media and was flashed across the world in a matter of hours. Speculation began to rise as to what the 35-year-old singer would do as the press pack pursued him. The media was desperate to speak to anyone who had been part of Michael's

NOT JUST BLACK OR WHITE

inner sanctum and swamped to the neighbouring village of Los Olivos. Chequebook journalism was very much the order of the day.

The alleged victim at the centre of it all was 13-year-old Jordy Chandler; he was questioned by the Los Angeles Child Services Department. His family issued a claim for damages. The police carried out hundreds of interviews with Jackson's friends and staff. Jackson denied all accusations of wrongdoing and vehemently proclaimed his innocence. Investigators searched Neverland Ranch, Hayvenhurst and other properties owned by the Jacksons.

It was during this difficult time that Michael began speaking regularly to Lisa Marie Presley on the telephone. The two of them had originally met in Las Vegas in 1974 when her father Elvis was in residence there. At that time their 10-year age gap meant that they had little in common, but in the early 1990s they were reintroduced to one another at a mutual friend's dinner party.

Michael Jackson still touring at the time was becoming emotionally fragile and was unable to continue with his world tour. The last date he played was 11 November 1993 in Mexico City. He contacted Elizabeth Taylor who together with her husband chartered a plane to be with Jackson. The party flew to Luton airport. The singer's management stated that, owing to increasing pressures the tour had been terminated. The star was suffering from exhaustion and had become dependent on painkillers for which he was seeking treatment. Investigations continued, potential witnesses were interviewed, and there were never any charges brought against Jackson. Michael Jackson settled with the Chandler family for an undisclosed fee the following January. The singer wanted to bring a swift end to the episode and allow a return to normality for everyone concerned.

13

A new start

MICHAEL JACKSON

A NEW START

At the start of 1994, Michael and Lisa Marie Presley's romance began to blossom. The couple went to see The Temptations play in Las Vegas in early February; observers said that they looked to be "into each other". Lisa Marie Presley, the only child of Elvis and Priscilla, had spent most of her 26 years in the spotlight. She had had a much more comfortable childhood than Jackson, but also had had her fair share of problems. Lisa Marie said that she probably "connected" with Michael because their lives were so different to that of ordinary people.

The couple's next high-profile outing was at

A NEW START

the Jackson Family Honours evening. The postponed event, produced by Jermaine, was an opportunity for the Jacksons to show a united family front and bestow 'honours' on their friends. Michael did not perform that evening.

After what seemed like a whirlwind romance, the couple tied the knot on Thursday, 26 May 1994. Lisa Marie's divorce from first husband Danny Keough had only been finalised 20 days earlier.

The couple were married in Dela Vego in the Dominican Republic. The ceremony that lasted a quarter of an hour was conducted in Spanish by Judge Francisco Alvarez Perez and translated by a lawyer. None of Michael Jackson's family or friends were invited. Thomas Keough, Lisa Marie's ex-brother-in-law, and a couple of Lisa Marie's friends witnessed the event.

Neither of the mothers-in-law, Priscilla nor Katherine, was happy about being denied the opportunity to buy new hats. The newly weds publicly refused to admit that they had been married. However speculation was rife and eventually the press obtained and printed a grainy photograph from the short ceremony. Upon their return to the States, the two spent most of their time in New York where Michael was working on

A NEW START

his latest album. The couple finally admitted to the marriage in August via a short statement issued by Michael's own record label; it also confirmed the new bride's name, Lisa Marie Presley-Jackson. The King of Pop had married the King's daughter. At the MTV Video Awards in September, the couple staged a very public display of affection. Their prolonged kiss captured the headlines for days to follow; some likened it to the screen kiss between Clark Cable and Vivian Leigh. This analogy particularly appealed to Jackson. He had always been a huge fan of the 1939 movie classic *Gone With The Wind*. Sixty years after the films producer, David O Selznick, won the Best Picture Oscar, Jackson bought the statue at Sotheby's for a whopping $1,542,500. This is highest price that anyone has ever paid for a piece of Hollywood memorabilia.

Michael unveiled his latest offering on 15 June 1995, it was a huge double album effort called *HIStory – Past, Present and Future Book 1*. It comprised 30 tunes, 15 classics and 15 new cuts. Sony gave the album the hard sell; statues of Michael Jackson were displayed across European cities. The King of Pop was striking a defiant stance, as the statue cruised down the Thames on

A NEW START

the back of a barge. The stunt confused blurry-eyed commuters when they saw a giant Michael Jackson passing through Tower Bridge.

Michael had been working with a range of producers and artists for this project. He collaborated with his little sister Janet for the single *Scream*. The single broke a long-standing record held by the Beatles by entering the US Billboard Hot 100 Chart at number five. The Beatles single *Let It Be* made its debut at number six in March 1970. Mark Romanek directed the stylised $7 million award-winning video that accompanied the single. Michael also joined forces with her legendary producers, Jimmy Jam and Terry Lewis. Other big names featured on the album include R Kelly, Boyz II Men, and Notorious BIG. The album reached in excess of 15 million global sales.

You Are Not Alone reached number one in the US and the UK charts. The poignant *Earth Song* addressed issues close to Michael's heart, the state of the planet, conservation concerns and the impact of dubious political decisions. It was while Jackson was performing this number at the 1996 Brit Awards that Pulp frontman Jarvis Cocker, invaded the stage. He stumbled around before

MICHAEL JACKSON

A NEW START

wiggling his bottom at the audience. Jackson's security dragged Cocker away. He spent the night at a police station before being released without charge. Cocker claimed that he was annoyed with Jackson portraying himself as a 'Christ-like figure'. Their record sales would later testify that both artists benefited from the incident.

While on the professional front, Michael Jackson's career was back on track, behind the scenes his personal life was taking a battering. Lisa Marie and Michael were growing further apart. Lisa Marie didn't enjoy the media attention she had to contend with as Mrs Michael Jackson. In the first few months of the marriage everything was 'normal', they went out to dinner with friends, spent quiet nights in, and had time to enjoy one another's company. Like her husband, Lisa Marie enjoyed her privacy. However, unlike Michael Jackson she had never really done anything to court the press. Lisa Marie resisted taking part in publicity opportunities, and prior to her Jackson marriage very rarely gave interviews. Lisa Marie was not really enjoying her new high profile position, or being part of the vast machine that surrounds Jackson. Eventually on the 18 January the pair announced that they were to split owing to their irreconcilable

A NEW START

differences. The divorce was finalised on 19 January 1996, 19 months after marrying.

Jackson threw himself into his work promoting *HIStory*, which in May picked up a record-breaking five World Music Awards. In September 1996 Jackson was back on the road again, with a 35-country world tour. An expectant audience of over 130,000 turned out to see Jackson's first show in Prague. Over 4.5 million people saw Jackson's concerts over its 80 dates around the world.

During the tour, the Jackson camp made a big announcement, Michael Jackson was going to become a daddy. Very few people had heard of the mother-to-be, Debbie Rowe. Rowe who was 37, had known Jackson since the early Eighties. She had been a nurse and receptionist at the dermatology clinic that Jackson attended. Rowe was very much an independent woman, she loved her work and she loved her Harley's. The couple were married on 14 November 1996, in a Sydney Hotel. Three months later, Debbie gave birth to the couple's first child, Prince Michael Joseph Jackson, Michael was present at the birth. Michael and Debbie were understandably overjoyed; Macaulay Culkin and Elizabeth Taylor landed one of their favourite roles

A NEW START

ever as the child's godparents. After the birth Prince stayed with Michael who was working in Paris at the time while Debbie did a 13-hour commute twice a month to spend time with them. This somewhat unconventional arrangement suited both parties, Debbie Rowe continued working at the surgery. She tried to carry on life as usual and felt that if Prince stayed with her, he would have to be looked after by nannies whilst she was at work. Being more or less his own boss, Michael spent most of his time his new son. His baby would accompany him to meetings, Michael fed him while taking conference calls and looking after other aspects of his corporation.

Never one to stay still for long, Jackson continued the *HIStory* world tour. He set off for the next leg of the tour in Germany on 31 May. Michael played the last date in the *HIStory* concert series in South Africa at the King's Park Stadium in October 1997.

Sony Music thought that there would be some mileage in a remix album. The result was *Blood On The Dance Floor L' HIStory In The Mix*. It was aimed at the young club-orientated market. It was released in April 1997 and recorded while Jackson was touring. Michael made the album 'on

A NEW START

the road', and in various studios around the world. The album had 18 tracks, 13 remixes and five new tunes. The title track, *Blood On The Dance Floor,* went to number one in the UK and despite poor promotion the album produced a very healthy 4 million in worldwide sales.

In May, Michael and his brothers were awarded on of their highest ever honours, when they were inducted into the Rock And Roll Hall Of Fame. The prestigious honour is only open to acts that have been around for quarter of a century. The original Jackson Five attended the ceremony, where Diana Ross presented the boys with the award. Berry Gordy joined the brothers on stage, and Michael Jackson paid tribute to his leadership and vision. Also honoured on that evening were The Bee Gees, Joni Mitchell and Crosby, Stills and Nash. The previous year one of the Jacksons' oldest and biggest fans was honoured, Gladys Knight.

As if Jackson had not been busy enough, he also found time to work with director Stan Winston (special effects make-up artist on *The Wiz*) on a short 38-minute sci-fi horror flick called *Ghosts*. The film, developed from a concept by writer Stephen King has Michael Jackson playing

MICHAEL JACKSON

five different roles. It premiered at the Cannes Film Festival two days after the Hall of Fame event and holds the world record for the longest music video ever made.

Debbie Rowe announced that she was pregnant for the second time in November 1997, saying that the child had been conceived whilst the couple were in Paris. Debbie gave birth on 3 April 1998, to a 7lb, 7oz baby girl, Paris Katherine Michael Jackson. Following the birth of their second child, Debbie and Michael who for various reasons had spent a lot of time apart, decided to go their separate ways. Mr and Mrs Jackson initiated divorce proceedings in October 1999. The split was amicable, and the children continued to live with their father at Neverland.

14

New millennium man

MICHAEL JACKSON

NEW MILLENNIUM MAN

M ichael Jackson spent much of 2000 working on his sixth solo album and becoming involved in more charity projects. Since 2000 Michael Jackson has retained the Guinness Book of Records title for the pop star that supports the most charities. Jackson is involved with 39 charity organisations, either giving them monetary donations, raising funds or support through association. Among those that he is linked with are Aids Project LA, American Cancer Society, Child Help USA, The Sickle Cell Research Foundation, Transafrica and Wish Granting.

With his recent personal problems, Jackson's

latest album was even more eagerly anticipated than normal. His fans and his Sony Music bosses were waiting to see if the twice-divorced, father-of-two really did have what it takes to produce the goods again. Having had the biggest-selling album of all time, it was always at the back of Michael's mind that he had to beat his own record. Throughout the years Michael Jackson's harshest critic has always been Michael Jackson. The better he does, the better he needs to do. In an effort to be innovative Jackson started to look towards the hottest young artists around.

The launch date for his long awaited follow up to *HIStory* kept being postponed, everyone was tight-lipped about the latest Jackson project. The suits at Sony seemed to have no idea when the album would be out, and the Jackson camp was not disclosing anything. Michael is a prolific writer, the majority of Michael's work is never released. The singer has stated that he writes in excess of 100 songs for each album in addition to reviewing submissions from commissioned composers. Reports emerged that the production costs were spiralling out of control, $20 million was being mooted. Only one thing was for sure, even before it had even been finished, it was the most expensive popular music album ever produced.

Michael was recruiting some of the most talented performers and producers that the industry had to offer. One such producer was Rodney Jerkins; he had worked with the Spice Girls, Puff Daddy, Toni Braxton, Destiny's Child and the Blackstreet Boys. Jackson also returned to his old favourite, tried-and-tested studio engineer Bruce Swedien of *Thriller* and *Dangerous* fame. Jackson reviewed more than 30 songs, but it was eventually reduced to 16. Other music industries megastars to be signed up were Carlos Santana, Missy Elliot, Boyz II Men, and R Kelly. Jerkins said that the new Jackson album was "banging hard" but still no release date was forthcoming. The speculation continued.

In March Michael popped over to England. When he touched down at Heathrow airport, Michael and his entourage, which included Macaulay Culkin called HMV's Oxford Street store with a request. Would they mind staying open a little longer so that Michael could do a little after hours shopping? The reply was swift and affirmative. Michael Jackson, who was on crutches after breaking two bones in his foot whilst at his Neverland Ranch, hobbled out of his

NEW MILLENNIUM MAN

limo and into the shop. Security was very tight as Jackson and Culkin browsed the stacks. His HMV outing made the BBC News on 5 March 2001 where they estimated that the total bill was approximately £1,500.

One of the reasons that Michael had made the journey across the pond was to fulfil the duty as best man at Uri Geller's 'wedding'. Uri Geller wanted to renew his vows to his wife of three decades, Hanna. Michael Jackson had been a fan of Uri Geller's ever since he witnessed his supernatural powers on a television programme.

Later that day Michael attended a fan convention at a packed Hammersmith Apollo, however, the main reason for the superstar's UK visit was to address the Oxford Student Union. Michael used the opportunity to promote his charity. Uri Geller, accompanied the superstar together with Rabbi Shmuley Boteach. The Jackson entourage received a rapturous welcome, although they were over three hours late. Twenty thousand people applied to attend the five hundred capacity chamber. In its 180 years the Oxford Union has attracted many diverse speakers including O J Simpson, Mother Teresa, Gerry Adams and Albert Einstein. Michael addressed the

NEW MILLENNIUM MAN

assembled forum: "Friends, I do not claim to have the academic expertise of other speakers who have addressed this hall, just as they could lay little claim at being adept at the moonwalk, and you know, Einstein in particular was really terrible at that." He went on to talk about his charity initiative Heal The Kids, and spoke of his own difficult childhood, and how he would like to see a fairer, more understanding world for children. The singer was tearful when he recalled some aspects of his own upbringing and stunned the crowd with his candour. Jackson received a mortar board, gown and his forth standing ovation of the evening at the end of his lecture.

He gave a thoughtful account of how his own children may view him in years to come. Michael also hinted at his relationship with his own father. It was one of the most considered public speeches that the entertainer has given.

The year 2001 promised to be busy for Jackson. With a proposed new album in the spring, a 43rd birthday in the summer, and a professional landmark to celebrate in the autumn.

This was the year that Michael Jackson celebrated his 30th year as a solo artist. He was determined to mark the occasion appropriately by

NEW MILLENNIUM MAN

throwing a seriously big bash. Billed as Michael Jackson: 30th Anniversary Celebration, The Solo Years, Jackson booked Madison Square Gardens and some showbiz pals to do a few turns. The two special Big Apple concerts were set for 7 and 10 September. David Gest produced the event, and it was here that he would meet his future wife, Liza Minnelli. Gest a renowned producer and promoter was a huge fan of Minnelli's mother, Judy Garland, and an avid collector of Garland memorabilia. When tickets finally went on sale, they were snapped up within hours. The tickets were priced from $200 for the cheap seats to $2,500 for the thrones. A row was sparked as some of the Jackson Brothers felt the cost prohibiting for their loyal fans. Rumours that the brothers were withdrawing from the show began to surface. Other controversy also served to increase interest in the concerts.

The 35,000 fans who turned up to the star-studded event were not to be disappointed. Everyone predicted that it would be lavish, and with a 300-member gospel choir, a 48 piece orchestra, 40 dancers and 12 backing singers, they were in for a treat. Some of the celebrity names to attend were Naomi Campbell, Samuel L Jackson, Kenny Rodgers and Sean P Diddy/Puff

MICHAEL JACKSON

NEW MILLENNIUM MAN

Daddy Combs. Looking every bit The King of Pop, Michael was seated in his 'Royal Box' with Elizabeth Taylor and Macaulay Culkin. Michael Jackson looked on as the cream of the industry paid him their dues. Entertainers from across the ages belted out their numbers. Veteran performers Liza Minnelli, Dionne Warwick, Gloria Estefan, Luther Vandross and Gladys Knight were all on hand to represent the old school. While current pop artists Usher, N'Sync, and Justin Timberlake appealed to the younger viewers.

The climax of the shows was the Jackson Five reunion. The boys performed a medley of the songs that had made them famous. It was exactly what the audience were waiting for. As the brothers performed together the years fell away, their magic and charisma was on display for all to see. The Jackson Five were the original boy-band, way before boy-bands had even been invented. Their choreographed moves took them back to Gary, Indiana, when they used to rehearse together in the living room under the watchful eye of their father. Joe looked on at them from the crowd.

Ultimately the night was a tribute to Michael Jackson and when it came down to it, everyone wanted to see him strut his legendary stuff.

MICHAEL JACKSON

NEW MILLENNIUM MAN

Michael knew exactly what they wanted and served up crowd-pleasers such as *Black Or White* accompanied by guitarist Slash, *The Way You Make Me Feel* performed with Britney Spears, and *Billie Jean* which was reminiscent of Michael's Motown Celebration performance. Attired with his necessary props, the rhinestone glove, the black fedora and the compulsory white socks, Jackson relished the moment and absorbed the atmosphere. Michael was in his element, doing what he does best. He was in the place where he felt most at home, the place where he has spent nearly four decades, performing for his adoring fans live on stage. The finale saw 40 of the world's biggest entertainers led by Quincy Jones perform *We Are The World* before receiving a standing ovation. Globally, an estimated 100 million viewers watched the event. At the exclusive after-show party was a *Wizard of Oz* themed affair at New York's Tavern on the Green, it was chicken vol-au-vents all round.

On the 10 September concert, Jackson performed his new single *Rock My World* from his long-awaited album. The tragic event that occurred in New York the following day rocked everyone's world, and would change the face of things forever. Prompted by the World Trade Centre attacks, he called upon his friends to sing on a charity record *What More Can I Give*. Among those who contributed their services were, Celine Dion, Mariah Carey, Beyonce Knowles, Usher, Ricky Martin and Carlos Santana. In October, Michael performed the song at the RFK Stadium in Washington DC, ticket sales raised $2.5 million for the Red Cross appeal, the Salvation Army and the Pentagon Fund. At the event Michael Jackson proclaimed: "You are not alone, you are in our hearts in our thoughts and in our prayers."

The new Michael Jackson album finally hit the streets at the end of October 2001. Entitled *Invincible* big things were expected of it. The new tracks were a mixture of mid-tempo romantic ballads and dance tunes. Some of the songs, for example *Butterflies,* were reminiscent of past successes such as *Rock With You*. Other cuts, such as *Heartbreaker*, *Unbreakable* and *Invincible* portrayed a more contemporary dance vibe. These contrasted well with the slow minimalist ballads like the silky smooth *Heaven Can Wait*. Jackson had used some of the finest R'n'B songwriter producers of the time including Baby Face and R Kelly. The album entered the US Billboard chart at number one and went on to clock up 4.5 million in its first fortnight. Final worldwide sales were under 10 million. Any other artist would have felt that a good result.

Unhappy with the overall support his new product was receiving Michael Jackson fell into dispute with Sony, his record bosses. He felt that they had not promoted the album strongly enough, he also felt let down by their lack of conviction and marketing. The label and their artist also had a different view of how much money should be allocated to the music videos. He didn't see eye to eye with Sony boss, Thomas D Mottola. At the time Tommy Mottola was a music mogul. His rags-to-riches tale began from a working class Italian America Family in New York's Bronx, to the lofty Manhattan Heights at Sony Entertainment. He is described as one of the most flamboyant music exec's ever. Mottola had been a singer and, as a child, won a music scholarship. So when he landed the Sony gig, it put him in the highly unusual position of being a music boss who actually knew something about music. He was the power behind Celine Dion and Jennifer Lopez's singing careers. His most memorable songbird is Mariah Carey who he married, but later divorced.

MICHAEL JACKSON

NEW MILLENNIUM MAN

In the summer of 2002, Michael Jackson led a protest outside Sony's London offices in Great Marlborough Street. Traffic was brought to a halt as hundreds of fans assembled outside the building. Word spread via Internet and text messages that the superstar was on his way. Michael Jackson arrived aloft a double-decker tourist bus and greeted his fans. Jackson led similar demonstrations in other European cities.

Earlier in the year Michael attended the wedding of Liza Minnelli and David Gest. Michael had been a childhood friend of Gest, they became neighbours when the Jacksons moved to their Hayvenhurst House. Jackson was honoured when he was approached to be the best man. Elizabeth Taylor and Mia Farrow were amongst those who fulfiled bridesmaids' duties. Liza strolled down the aisle to the strains of Natalie Cole singing *Unforgettable*. The Gest's guest list was an eclectic mix that read like a who's who in entertainment. It included Diana Ross, the wholesome Donny Osmond, camp comic Graham Norton, silver screen stars Janet Leigh and Mickey Rooney, ex-soap star Martine McCutcheon (also a bridesmaid) and actor David Hassalhoff. Sixteen months after their special day Liza and David separated.

15

The road ahead

THE ROAD AHEAD

I n the same month that Michael Jackson celebrated his 44th birthday, he also announced the birth of his third child, Prince Michael Jackson II, the child was approximately six months old at the time. Mystery still surrounds this child. Michael has not disclosed the date of the birth or the identity of the surrogate mother, owing to contractual restraints. Michael lives with and has custody of all of his three children. All that is known is that Prince Michael II is a very healthy, very happy, very normal young boy. Michael Jackson nicknamed his new son Blanket Jackson – equating the term 'blanket' to showing

THE ROAD AHEAD

love and caring – using it as a term of endearment. When in public Michael keeps his children's faces covered. They either wear thin veils, or masks. The entertainer believes that by doing this, he can maintain their privacy and thereby reduce any possibility of kidnapping.

In 2003 Granada Television produced a documentary called *Tonight with Trevor Macdonald: Living With Michael Jackson*. Screened in February on ITV 1, the film presented by Martin Bashir followed Michael Jackson over a period of eight months. Journalist Martin Bashir was famed for his BAFTA-award-winning interview with Diana, Princess of Wales, during which she coined the title 'Queen of Hearts'. The current affairs journalist had been pursuing an interview with the superstar for five years. Bashir's wishes were granted after Michael contacted his friend Uri Geller for his opinions. Bashir was afforded a no-holds-barred access-all-areas interviews with Michael. During the two-hour programme viewers were invited into Jackson's amazing Neverland home.

Jackson was shown with his children on expeditions visiting the zoo, on a shopping spree, accepting awards and entertaining underprivileged children on his ranch. The singer also revealed his

THE ROAD AHEAD

favourite pastimes and his composition process. He also spoke of his father Joe, describing how he used to beat the boys with his belt as they rehearsed their routines. Michael revealed how Joe Jackson terrified and physically bullied his sons.

Michael Jackson was not happy with the programme when he saw the preview. The singer felt that Bashir had given a misleading portrait of him; partly due to convenient editing, it didn't paint him in a good light. Michael decided to strike back with his own film, *Michael Jackson: The Footage You Were Never Meant To See*. It featured footage that Jackson's own team had recorded along with interviews with other members of Michael's family and ex-wife, Debbie Rowe. It presented a unified front and showed that Martin Bashir seemed to be somewhat disingenuous with regard to his voiceovers during the show. Jackson also felt that the innocent feelings that he felt for children that had stayed with him at Neverland had been misinterpreted in the film.

However, the main cause of concern was a piece conducted with Michael in the presence of a 13-year-old boy. The boy who was suffering from cancer openly admitted that he had stayed with Michael. Martin Bashir questioned whether or not

MICHAEL JACKSON

THE ROAD AHEAD

Jackson's behaviour was appropriate. Troubling rumblings were beginning to surface.

Sony set about putting together an album release for later in the year, Michael Jackson's *Number Ones*. The compilation album, which does exactly what it says on the label, featured three decades of the superstar's number one hits. It had all of the familiar favourites. The guaranteed instant classic album was an audible CV of Michael Jackson's long running career. It contains a special and exclusive live rendition of *Ben*. The unmissable record-breaking *Thriller* LP is represented by *Billie Jean* and *Beat It*. Michael's 1987 *Bad* LP also gets an airing with *The Way You Make Me Feel*, *Dirty Diana* and *Smooth Criminal* making an appearance. The album is brought up to date with *Rock My World* from *Invincible*. One unexpected surprise is the R Kelly penned retro ballad *One More Chance*. This track was actually written for the *Invincible* album, but never made it on to the final edit.

When the album was released in America on 18 November 2003, it coincided with the day the police officers raided Michael Jackson's Neverland ranch. Their investigations had lasted two months but somehow the events coincidentally clashed.

MICHAEL JACKSON

THE ROAD AHEAD

The police were following up allegations made against the star. The following day the police issued an arrest warrant for the entertainer, his fans in the US, UK, Tokyo and Tel Aviv held vigils and voiced their concerns. They feared it was a witch-hunt and the high-profile star may not be treated fairly. People wondered whether these allegations would affect Michael Jackson's popularity among ordinary people. Michael Jackson was formally charged with seven counts of child abuse on the 18 December 2003. From day one he has always maintained his innocence. The case will soon go to trial.

This has been a difficult few years for Michael Jackson, failed marriages, fallouts with his record company as well as the high-profile arrest. It would seem an impossible trap to escape from for the boy from Gary. However Jackson has managed to survive, regroup and reinvent himself many times. He believes in himself and has profound faith. He knows that truth will always ultimately prevail. It's impossible and futile to predict what the future holds for Michael. He embodies a world of contradictions, off-stage Michael Jackson is shy and unassuming, on-stage he is a dominant presence, commanding

THE ROAD AHEAD

an audience of thousands. Although in the public eye for nearly 50 years no one seems to know the real highly complex Michael Jackson, but his achievements speak for themselves.

He is genuinely altruistic, although he has amassed a considerable fortune he gets as much pleasure from giving it away. Business-wise Jackson has his fingers in lots of pies, but he is most happy doing the thing that he loves to do the best, entertain. Nobody can or will ever be able to entertain the way that Michael Jackson entertains. His performances encompass a lifetime of experience. He provokes a reaction like no other. Michael has sung and danced his way in to the record books during the past four decades and still remains the most famous man on the planet. It is a telling testimony by anyone's standards. His influence, his music, and his magic will live forever. There has never been and there will never be another Michael Jackson.

MICHAEL JACKSON

DISCOGRAPHY – ALBUMS

Michael Jackson solo albums

Got To Be There (1972)

Ben (1972)

Music & Me (1973)

Forever, Michael (1975)

The Best Of Michael Jackson (1975)

Off The Wall (1979)

One Day In Your Life (1981)

Thriller (1982)

Farewell My Summer Love (May 1984)

Bad (1987)

Dangerous (1991)

HIStory: Past, Present, and Future Book I (1995)

Blood On The Dance Floor: HIStory In The Mix (1997)

Invincible (2001)

Greatest Hits - HIStory Volume I (2001)

Number Ones (2003)

DISCOGRAPHY – ALBUMS

Jackson Five Albums

Joyful Jukebox Music (1976)

Moving Violation (1975)

Dancing Machine (1974)

Get it together (1974)

Skywriter (1973)

Lookin' trough the windows (1972)

Goin' back to Indiana (1971)

Maybe Tomorrow (1971)

Christmas Album (1970)

Third Album (1970)

ABC (1970)

Diana Ross

presents the Jackson 5

1969-

Pre-History (1996)

(Last edition of the Steeltown Recordings 1968)

The Jacksons' albums

2300 Jackson Street (1989)

Victory (1984)

Live (1981)

Triumph (1980)

Destiny (1978)

Goin' Places (1977)

The Jacksons (1976)

BIOGRAPHIES

OTHER BOOKS IN THE SERIES

Also available in the series:

OTHER BOOKS IN THE SERIES

JENNIFER ANISTON

She's been a Friend to countless millions worldwide, and overcame numerous hurdles to rise to the very top of her field. From a shy girl with a dream of being a famous actress, through being reduced to painting scenery for high school plays, appearing in a series of flop TV shows and one rather bad movie, Jennifer Aniston has persevered, finally finding success at the very top of the TV tree.

Bringing the same determination that got her a part on the world's best-loved TV series to her attempts at a film career, she's also worked her way from rom-com cutie up to serious, respected actress and box office draw, intelligently combining indie, cult and comedy movies into a blossoming career which looks set to shoot her to the heights of Hollywood's A-list. She's also found love with one of the world's most desirable men. Is Jennifer Aniston the ultimate Hollywood Renaissance woman? It would seem she's got more than a shot at such a title, as indeed, she seems to have it all, even if things weren't always that way. Learn all about Aniston's rise to fame in this compelling biography.

OTHER BOOKS IN THE SERIES

DAVID BECKHAM

This book covers the amazing life of the boy from East London who has not only become a world class footballer and the captain of England, but also an idol to millions, and probably the most famous man in Britain.

His biography tracks his journey, from the playing fields of Chingford to the Bernabau. It examines how he joined his beloved Manchester United and became part of a golden generation of talent that led to United winning trophies galore.

Beckham's parallel personal life is also examined, as he moved from tongue-tied football-obsessed kid to suitor of a Spice Girl, to one half of Posh & Becks, the most famous celebrity couple in Britain – perhaps the world. His non-footballing activities, his personal indulgences and changing styles have invited criticism, and even abuse, but his football talent has confounded the critics, again and again.

The biography looks at his rise to fame and his relationship with Posh, as well as his decision to leave Manchester for Madrid. Has it affected his relationship with Posh? What will the latest controversy over his sex life mean for celebrity's royal couple? And will he come back to play in England again?

OTHER BOOKS IN THE SERIES

GEORGE CLOONEY

The tale of George Clooney's astonishing career is an epic every bit as riveting as one of his blockbuster movies. It's a story of tenacity and determination, of fame and infamy, a story of succeeding on your own terms regardless of the risks. It's also a story of emergency rooms, batsuits, tidal waves and killer tomatoes, but let's not get ahead of ourselves.

Born into a family that, by Sixties' Kentucky standards, was dripping with show business glamour, George grew up seeing the hard work and heartache that accompanied a life in the media spotlight.

By the time stardom came knocking for George Clooney, it found a level-headed and mature actor ready and willing to embrace the limelight, while still indulging a lifelong love of partying and practical jokes. A staunchly loyal friend and son, a bachelor with a taste for the high life, a vocal activist for the things he believes and a born and bred gentleman; through failed sitcoms and blockbuster disasters, through artistic credibility and box office success, George Clooney has remained all of these things...and much, much more. Prepare to meet Hollywood's most fascinating megastar in this riveting biography.

OTHER BOOKS IN THE SERIES

BILLY CONNOLLY

In a 2003 London Comedy Poll to find Britain's favourite comedian, Billy Connolly came out on top. It's more than just Billy Connolly's all-round comic genius that puts him head and shoulders above the rest. Connolly has also proved himself to be an accomplished actor with dozens of small and big screen roles to his name. In 2003, he could be seen in *The Last Samurai* with Tom Cruise.

Connolly has also cut the mustard in the USA, 'breaking' that market in a way that chart-topping pop groups since The Beatles and the Stones have invariably failed to do, let alone mere stand-up comedians. Of course, like The Beatles and the Stones, Billy Connolly has been to the top of the pop charts too with D.I.V.O.R.C.E. in 1975.

On the way he's experienced heartache of his own with a difficult childhood and a divorce of his own, found the time and energy to bring up five children, been hounded by the press on more than one occasion, and faced up to some considerable inner demons. But Billy Connolly is a survivor. Now in his 60s, he's been in show business for all of 40 years, and 2004 finds him still touring. This exciting biography tells the story an extraordinary entertainer.

OTHER BOOKS IN THE SERIES

ROBERT DE NIRO

Robert De Niro is cinema's greatest chameleon. Snarling one minute, smirking the next, he's straddled Hollywood for a quarter of a century, making his name as a serious character actor, in roles ranging from psychotic taxi drivers to hardened mobsters. The scowls and pent-up violence may have won De Niro early acclaim but, ingeniously, he's now playing them for laughs, poking fun at the tough guy image he so carefully cultivated. Ever the perfectionist, De Niro holds nothing back on screen, but in real life he is a very private man – he thinks of himself as just another guy doing a job. Some job, some guy. There's more to the man than just movies. De Niro helped New York pick itself up after the September 11 terrorist attacks on the Twin Towers by launching the TriBeCa Film Festival and inviting everyone downtown. He runs several top-class restaurants and has dated some of the most beautiful women in the world, least of all supermodel Naomi Campbell. Now in his 60s, showered with awards and a living legend, De Niro's still got his foot on the pedal. There are six, yes six, films coming your way in 2004. In this latest biography, you'll discover all about his latest roles and the life of this extraordinary man.

OTHER BOOKS IN THE SERIES

MICHAEL DOUGLAS

Douglas may have been a shaggy-haired member of a hippy commune in the Sixties but just like all the best laidback, free-loving beatniks, he's gone on to blaze a formidable career, in both acting and producing.

In a career that has spanned nearly 40 years so far, Douglas has produced a multitude of hit movies including the classic *One Flew Over The Cuckoo's Nest* and *The China Syndrome* through to box office smashes such as Starman and *Face/Off*.

His acting career has been equally successful – from *Romancing The Stone* to *Wall Street* to *Fatal Attraction*, Douglas's roles have shown that he isn't afraid of putting himself on the line when up there on the big screen.

His relationship with his father; his stay in a top clinic to combat his drinking problem; the breakdown of his first marriage; and his publicised clash with the British media have all compounded to create the image of a man who's transformed himself from being the son of Hollywood legend Kirk Douglas, into Kirk Douglas being the dad of Hollywood legend, Michael Douglas.

OTHER BOOKS IN THE SERIES

HUGH GRANT

He's the Oxford fellow who stumbled into acting, the middle-class son of a carpet salesman who became famous for bumbling around stately homes and posh weddings. The megastar actor who claims he doesn't like acting, but has appeared in over 40 movies and TV shows.

On screen he's romanced a glittering array of Hollywood's hottest actresses, and tackled medical conspiracies and the mafia. Off screen he's hogged the headlines with his high profile girlfriend as well as finding lifelong notoriety after a little Divine intervention in Los Angeles.

Hugh Grant is Britain's biggest movie star, an actor whose talent for comedy has often been misjudged by those who assume he simply plays himself.

From bit parts in Nottingham theatre, through comedy revues at the Edinburgh Fringe, and on to the top of the box office charts, Hugh has remained constant – charming, witty and ever so slightly sarcastic, obsessed with perfection and performance while winking to his audience as if to say: "This is all awfully silly, isn't it?" Don't miss this riveting biography.

OTHER BOOKS IN THE SERIES

NICOLE KIDMAN

On 23 March 2003 Nicole Kidman won the Oscar for Best Actress for her role as Virginia Woolf in *The Hours*. That was the night that marked Nicole Kidman's acceptance into the upper echelons of Hollywood royalty. She had certainly come a long way from the 'girlfriend' roles she played when she first arrived in Hollywood – in films such as *Billy Bathgate* and *Batman Forever* – although even then she managed to inject her 'pretty girl' roles with an edge that made her acting stand out. And she was never merely content to be Mrs Cruise, movie star's wife. Although she stood dutifully behind her then husband in 1993 when he was given his star on the Hollywood Walk of Fame, Nicole got a star of her own 10 years later, in 2003.

Not only does Nicole Kidman have stunning good looks and great pulling power at the box office, she also has artistic credibility. But Nicole has earned the respect of her colleagues, working hard and turning in moving performances from a very early age. Although she dropped out of school at 16, no one doubts the intelligence and passion that are behind the fiery redhead's acting career, which includes television and stage work, as well as films. Find out how Kidman became one of Hollywood's most respected actresses in this compelling biography.

OTHER BOOKS IN THE SERIES

JENNIFER LOPEZ

There was no suggestion that the Jennifer Lopez of the early Nineties would become the accomplished actress, singer and icon that she is today. Back then she was a dancer on the popular comedy show *In Living Color* – one of the Fly Girls, the accompaniment, not the main event. In the early days she truly was Jenny from the block; the Bronx native of Puerto Rican descent – another hopeful from the east coast pursuing her dreams in the west.

Today, with two marriages under her belt, three multi-platinum selling albums behind her and an Oscar-winning hunk as one of her ex-boyfriends, she is one of the most talked about celebrities of the day. Jennifer Lopez is one of the most celebrated Hispanic actresses of all time.

Her beauty, body and famous behind, are lusted after by men and envied by women throughout the world. She has proven that she can sing, dance and act. Yet her critics dismiss her as a diva without talent. And the criticisms are not just about her work, some of them are personal. But what is the reality? Who is Jennifer Lopez, where did she come from and how did get to where she is now? This biography aims to separate fact from fiction to reveal the real Jennifer Lopez.

OTHER BOOKS IN THE SERIES

MADONNA

Everyone thought they had Madonna figured out in early 2003. The former Material Girl had become Maternal Girl, giving up on causing controversy to look after her two children and set up home in England with husband Guy Ritchie. The former wild child had settled down and become respectable. The new Madonna would not do anything to shock the establishment anymore, she'd never do something like snogging both Britney Spears and Christina Aguilera at the MTV Video Music Awards... or would she?

Of course she would. Madonna has been constantly reinventing herself since she was a child, and her ability to shock even those who think they know better is both a tribute to her business skills and the reason behind her staying power. Only Madonna could create gossip with two of the current crop of pop princesses in August and then launch a children's book in September. In fact, only Madonna would even try.

In her 20-year career she has not just been a successful pop singer, she is also a movie star, a business woman, a stage actress, an author and a mother. Find out all about this extraordinary modern-day icon in this new compelling biography.

OTHER BOOKS IN THE SERIES

BRAD PITT

From the launch pad that was his scene stealing turn in *Thelma And Louise* as the sexual-enlightening bad boy. To his character-driven performances in dramas such as *Legends of the Fall* through to his Oscar-nominated work in *Twelve Monkeys* and the dark and razor-edged Tyler Durden in *Fight Club*, Pitt has never rested on his laurels. Or his good looks.

And the fact that his love life has garnered headlines all over the world hasn't hindered Brad Pitt's profile away from the screen either – linked by the press to many women, his relationships with the likes of Juliette Lewis and Gwyneth Paltrow. Then of course, in 2000, we had the Hollywood fairytale ending when he tied the silk knot with Jennifer Aniston.

Pitt's impressive track record as a superstar, sex symbol *and* credible actor looks set to continue as he has three films lined up for release over the next year – as Achilles in the Wolfgang Peterson-helmed Troy; Rusty Ryan in the sequel *Ocean's Twelve* and the titular Mr Smith in the thriller *Mr & Mrs Smith* alongside Angelina Jolie. Pitt's ever-growing success shows no signs of abating. Discover all about Pitt's meteoric rise from rags to riches in this riveting biography.

OTHER BOOKS IN THE SERIES

SHANE RICHIE

Few would begrudge the current success of 40-year-old Shane Richie. To get where he is today, Shane has had a rather bumpy roller coaster ride that has seen the hard working son of poor Irish immigrants endure more than his fair share of highs and lows – financially, professionally and personally.

In the space of four decades he has amused audiences at school plays, realised his childhood dream of becoming a Pontins holiday camp entertainer, experienced homelessness, beat his battle with drink, became a million-aire then lost the lot. He's worked hard and played hard.

When the producers of *EastEnders* auditioned Shane for a role in the top TV soap, they decided not to give him the part, but to create a new character especially for him. That character was Alfie Moon, manager of the Queen Vic pub, and very quickly Shane's TV alter ego has become one of the most popular soap characters in Britain. This biography is the story of a boy who had big dreams and never gave up on turning those dreams into reality.

OTHER BOOKS IN THE SERIES

JONNY WILKINSON

"There's 35 seconds to go, this is the one. It's coming back for Jonny Wilkinson. He drops for World Cup glory. It's over! He's done it! Jonny Wilkinson is England's Hero yet again…"

That memorable winning drop kick united the nation, and lead to the start of unprecedented victory celebrations throughout the land. In the split seconds it took for the ball to leave his boot and slip through the posts, Wilkinson's life was to change forever. It wasn't until three days later, when the squad flew back to Heathrow and were met with a rapturous reception, that the enormity of their win, began to sink in.

Like most overnight success stories, Wilkinson's journey has been a long and dedicated one. He spent 16 years 'in rehearsal' before achieving his finest performance, in front of a global audience of 22 million, on that rainy evening in Telstra Stadium, Sydney.

But how did this modest self-effacing 24-year-old become England's new number one son? This biography follows Jonny's journey to international stardom. Find out how he caught the rugby bug, what and who his earliest influences were and what the future holds for our latest English sporting hero.

OTHER BOOKS IN THE SERIES

ROBBIE WILLIAMS

Professionally, things can't get much better for Robbie Williams. In 2002 he signed the largest record deal in UK history when he re-signed with EMI. The following year he performed to over 1.5 million fans on his European tour, breaking all attendance records at Knebworth with three consecutive sell-out gigs.

Since going solo Robbie Williams has achieved five No.1 hit singles, five No. 1 hit albums; 10 Brits and 3 Ivor Novello awards. When he left the highly successful boy band Take That in 1995 his future seemed far from rosy. He got off to a shaky start. His nemesis, Gary Barlow, had already recorded two No.1 singles and the press had virtually written Williams off. But then in December 1997, he released his Christmas single, *Angels.*

Angels re-launched his career – it remained in the Top 10 for 11 weeks. Since then Robbie has gone from strength to strength, both as a singer and a natural showman. His live videos are a testament to his performing talent and his promotional videos are works of art.

This biography tells of Williams' journey to the top – stopping off on the way to take a look at his songs, his videos, his shows, his relationships, his rows, his record deals and his demons.